STARK

Abitur *Skript*

Englisch

Gymnasium • Gesamtschule
Niedersachsen

STARK

Bildnachweis:

Krankenhaus S. 9: © Marco's studio/shutterstock
weiße und rote Rose S. 59: © Sodacan/wikipedia, CC BY-SA 3.0
weitere Abbildungen und grafische Darstellungen: © Redaktion

www.stark-verlag.de

Inhalt

Richard III (zusätzlich für eA)

Autor: Rainer Jacob

Vorwort

Liebe Schülerinnen und Schüler,

dieses handliche Skript bietet Ihnen umfassende Informationen zu allen **verbindlichen Materialien** (Pflichtlektüren und -filme), die Sie für die **Abiturprüfung 2021** im Fach Englisch kennen müssen.
Dank der knappen, übersichtlichen Darstellung eignet es sich besonders zur Auffrischung und Wiederholung des Prüfungsstoffs kurz vor dem Abitur:

- Anhand der Kennzeichnung im Inhaltsverzeichnis können Sie ersehen, welche Materialien sowohl im **grundlegenden** als auch im **erhöhten Anforderungsniveau** verbindlich sind, welche nur für das erhöhte Niveau vorausgesetzt werden und welche zusätzlich an **Beruflichen Gymnasien** zu behandeln sind.
- Jedes Kapitel enthält die wichtigsten **Fakten** zum Text bzw. Film, eine **Zusammenfassung der Handlung** und eine Übersicht über die zentralen **Figuren**.
- Unter „Themes and interpretation“ finden Sie **Interpretationsansätze** zu den Werken, die Ihnen bei der Bearbeitung von möglichen Abituraufgaben helfen können. Gerade im dritten Teil der Textaufgabe wird häufig von Ihnen verlangt, inhaltliche Aspekte aus dem Prüfungstext (den Sie im Abitur erstmals zu Gesicht bekommen) zu den verpflichtenden Materialien (die Sie aus dem Unterricht kennen) in Bezug zu setzen. Die in diesem Skript behandelten Themen orientieren sich an den vom Niedersächsischen Kultusministerium festgelegten „verbindlichen Unterrichtsaspekten“ und sind so für die Abiturprüfung besonders relevant (siehe Übersicht auf der folgenden Seite).
- Zahlreiche **Schaubilder** und **Beispiele** helfen Ihnen, sich das Gelernte besser einzuprägen.

Viel Erfolg beim Lernen mit diesem Skript und im Abitur!

Rainer Jacob

Kerncurriculum und verbindliche Materialien

Die folgende Tabelle veranschaulicht, wo sich die verbindlichen Materialien im Kerncurriculum Englisch verorten lassen. Die linke Spalte enthält die zentralen Themen des Kerncurriculums; rechts finden Sie die Pflichtlektüren/-filme mit den verbindlichen Unterrichtsaspekten.

Individual and Society	
identity	**"Two Kinds" and "The Child":** (ethnic) identity, growing up
ethnic, cultural and linguistic diversity	***Crash:*** ethnic and cultural diversity
gender and sexual diversity	
Science and Technology	
chances and risks	***Never Let Me Go:*** ethics of science
visions of the future	***Never Let Me Go:*** dystopian literature, visions of the future
the media, e. g. the influence of the media on public opinion and personal life	
the digital revolution	
Globalisation	
effects on the world of work	
impact on personal lives	
global responsibility concerning e. g. politics, the environment, economy	
English as a global language	
Beliefs, Values and Norms in Society: Tradition and Change	
Britishness	
the American experience	**"Two Kinds" and "The Child":** The American Dream ***Hidden Figures:*** The American Dream, discrimination and equality in the world of work ***Crash:*** beliefs, values and norms in society
postcolonial / neo-colonial experiences	
migration effects on the world of work	
Shakespeare (nur eA)	
the world that made him modern adaptations	***Richard III:*** the pursuit of power, the role(s) of women, fate vs. free will

Never Let Me Go

1 Key facts about the novel

- **author:** Kazuo Ishiguro (*1954 in Nagasaki, Japan; family moved to England in 1960), Man Booker Prize for his third novel *The Remains of the Day* (1989), Nobel Prize in Literature (2017)
- **year of publication:** 2005
- **awards:** nominated for the Booker Prize (2005), named the best novel of 2005 by *TIME* magazine
- **adaptations:** British film adaptation directed by Mark Romanek (2010), Japanese television drama adaptation (2016)
- **genre:** dystopian science fiction novel
- **setting:** England
- **time:** late 1990s
- **narrative perspective:** first-person narration; main character Kathy H. tells the story in retrospect; as the novel follows Kathy's memory, the narration is not strictly chronological, but rather episodic and guided by association
- **structure:** 23 chapters; Part One: 1–9 (boarding school Hailsham), Part Two: 10–17 (the Cottages), Part Three: 18–23 (recovery centres; different parts of the country)
- **content:** The novel tells the story of three friends, Kathy, Ruth and Tommy, who are raised and educated in a boarding school called Hailsham. What is not immediately apparent to the reader: all students at Hailsham are clones, destined to donate their organs as young adults in order to prolong the lives of ordinary humans. Every "donor" receives care from a designated "carer" (a clone who has not yet begun the donation process) until they die ("complete").
- **explanation of the title:** name of Kathy's favourite song on a cassette tape

Who's Who in *Never Let Me Go*

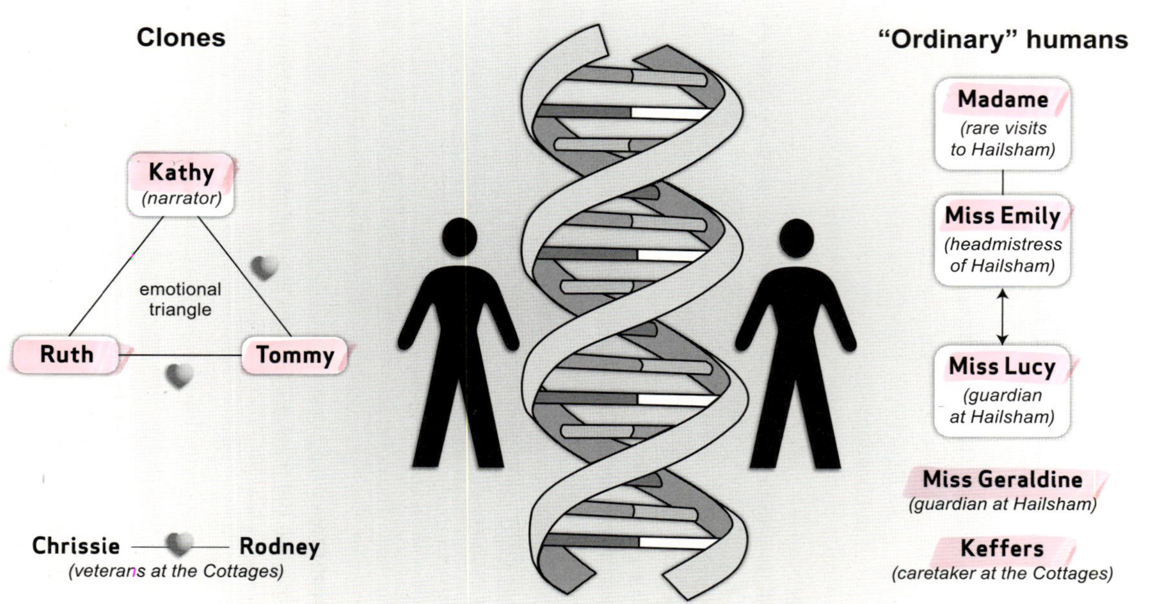

2 Plot

Part One

Chapter 1

- narrator Kathy H. introduces herself: she is 31, has been a "carer" for over 11 years
- travelling around the country, she recalls episodes from her childhood at Hailsham
- her best friends are Ruth and Tommy, who is often bullied by his schoolmates and tends to have fits of rage as a result
- **Background** (what the reader does not know yet):
  the students at Hailsham are clones who are raised to provide ("donate") organs for transplantation to non-clones who need them

Chapter 2

- the teachers at Hailsham put special importance on the students' efforts in arts, poetry and creativity
- Tommy's schoolmates mock his paintings (elephant); he gives up trying to be creative
- Tommy is relieved when Miss Lucy tells him that there is nothing wrong with not being creative; his tantrums stop
- **Background** (what the reader does not know yet):
  Miss Lucy will later revoke her statement, as she realises creativity at Hailsham does matter

Chapter 3

- Tommy and Kathy try to make sense of Miss Lucy's hints that creativity is not so important and that the students are taught too little about donations
- occasionally, a strange woman, called Madame, arrives and chooses the best pictures for her "Gallery"
- **Background** (what the reader does not know yet):
  Madame collects the pictures to prove that the clones have feelings

Chapter 4

- the students ask Miss Lucy about Madame's Gallery
- she tells them it is a for a good reason which she cannot explain
- Ruth and Kathy become friends when Ruth invites Kathy to ride one of her invisible horses
- Ruth lets Kathy be one of her "secret guards" for Miss Geraldine, her favourite guardian

Chapter 5

- Ruth suspects a plot to kidnap Miss Geraldine
- three years later: Kathy uncovers Ruth's lie about a pencil case which Ruth hinted she had been given by Miss Geraldine
- **Background** (what the reader does not know yet):
  these episodes illustrate the complicated relationship between Ruth and Kathy which is to continue in their adult lives

Chapter 6

- Kathy's cassette *Songs After Dark* by Judy Bridgewater (1956) contains her favourite song "Never Let Me Go"
- Kathy dances to the song, pretending to hold a baby in her arm; she is being watched by Madame, who sobs
- one day, the tape gets lost → years later, Tommy and Kathy find another copy of the tape in a shop in Norfolk and buy it
- in one of her lessons Miss Emily had called Norfolk the "lost corner" of England → students believe Norfolk is the place where all objects lost in England are brought (like a lost-and-found office)
- **Background** (what the reader does not know yet):
  Norfolk symbolises the hope that lost things can be recovered

Chapter 7

- some boys talk about their dream of becoming actors → Miss Lucy tells students their futures are determined (donate their vital organs)
- in Miss Emily's lessons, the topics of donation and sex are usually dealt with together (possibly to distract from the topic of donation)
- (older) students joke about donations

Chapter 8

- Ruth and Tommy are a couple
- Kathy is prepared to have sex with Harry C. "next summer"
- Ruth and Tommy split up

Chapter 9

- Kathy gives up her sex plans with Harry C. after a friend tells her that she might become Tommy's next girlfriend
- Ruth asks Kathy for help to get back together with Tommy again; Ruth and Tommy reunite, Kathy is back in Ruth's good books
- Tommy reveals that Miss Lucy reversed her advice about artwork
- Miss Lucy leaves Hailsham
- **Background** (what the reader does not know yet): Miss Lucy is frustrated about her role; she feels pity for the students

Part Two

Chapter 10

- Kathy, Tommy and Ruth move to the Cottages, an old farmhouse
- more independence, no guardians, caretaker Keffers
- they live there together with older residents ("veterans") and students from other institutions
- veteran couples imitate their peculiar behaviour from TV programmes
- increasing tension between Kathy and Ruth; Kathy is different from Ruth in as much as she does not copy the mannerisms from TV

Chapter 11

- new relationship with Ruth: quarrels and confident conversations
- Kathy tells Ruth about her one-night-stands at the Cottages and the urge she feels "down there"; Ruth suggests that Kathy's sexual urges are unusual
- other residents of the Cottages do not have collections of artwork from school → Kathy still has hers; Ruth gives hers away to charity
- no one talks about students who recently left the Cottages

Chapter 12

- explanation of the theory of "possibles" (the normal persons the students were copied from)
- Chrissie and Rodney claim to have spotted Ruth's possible working in an office in Norfolk
- newcomers think about future jobs ("dream futures"), but Kathy remembers Miss Lucy's information (no future)
- Ruth sees an advert of people working in an office → her dream job
- all five go on a trip to Norfolk to search for Ruth's possible

Chapter 13

- while in Norfolk, Rodney mentions a rumour that loving couples can apply for a deferral (donations three or four years later)
- Tommy says he doesn't know anything about this matter but Ruth insinuates the rumour is true
- **Background** (what the reader does not know yet):
  Ruth gives a wrong impression of Hailsham students; they were never told about deferrals

Chapter 14

- they spot Ruth's possible (a woman around fifty) working in an office and follow her into a gallery
- a closer look makes them decide she is not Ruth's possible
- Ruth is disappointed and upset

Chapter 15

- Tommy and Kathy wander around the city on their own; they buy Kathy's favourite tape by Judy Bridgewater
- Tommy's theory: there is a connection between deferrals and the Gallery (the paintings are used to determine whether couples are really in love)
- he has taken up artwork again, drawing imaginary animals
- Kathy admits that she keeps looking for her possible in porn magazines (to explain her strong sexual urges)

Chapter 16

- more talk about deferrals; Kathy and Tommy do not take part
- Tommy shows Kathy his drawings of tiny animals
- Ruth mocks "Tommy's big Gallery theory" and his paintings; Kathy feels like letting Tommy down

Chapter 17

- Kathy, Ruth and Tommy are not as close as they used to be
- Ruth tells Kathy that she and Tommy might not be a couple forever, but that Tommy would never see Kathy as a "proper girlfriend"
- Kathy decides to apply for training to become a carer
- **Background** (what the reader does not know yet):
  turning point in the relationship of the old friends Kathy, Ruth and Tommy

Part Three

Chapter 18

- it becomes clear that Hailsham has been closed
- Kathy becomes Ruth's carer; their relationship is very tense at first
- Ruth would like to see a stranded boat near a centre where Tommy is a donor; they arrange a visit with Tommy

Chapter 19

- Kathy and Ruth meet Tommy at the recovery centre
- together they drive to the abandoned boat in the marshes
- on their way back, they pass a poster showing an open-plan office, remembering Ruth's dream of working in an office one day
- Ruth asks Kathy to forgive her for claiming that Kathy's sexual urges were unusual and for keeping Tommy and Kathy apart → urges them to get a deferral and gives them Madame's address
- after the trip, the relationship between Ruth and Kathy improves
- Ruth dies after her second donation; Kathy promises her to become Tommy's carer

Chapter 20

- Kathy becomes Tommy's carer after his third donation
- they become a couple and begin to have sex
- Kathy reports having seen Madame; they plan to visit her and ask for a deferral

Chapter 21

- Kathy and Tommy visit Madame (aka Marie-Claude)
- Tommy explains his "Gallery theory", offers to show Madame his drawings
- Madame calls on Miss Emily to speak to Tommy and Kathy

Chapter 22

- Miss Emily explains that Hailsham (and her "Gallery") was an experiment to demonstrate that clones had souls
- in other institutions clones were raised in much worse conditions
- people became used to diseases being cured; they did not want to know where organs came from and tried to convince themselves that clones were less than human
- Morningdale scandal: scientist Morningdale created clones with enhanced genetic characteristics
- Miss Lucy had wanted to tell the clones the whole truth about their fates, whereas Miss Emily wanted to give them a sheltered childhood by keeping the horrible truth from them → on the way home, Tommy says he thinks that Miss Lucy was right; gets out of the car and screams

Chapter 23

- Tommy's fourth donation is ahead → more afraid of surviving and suffering than of "completing" (dying)
- does not want Kathy as carer any longer so that she doesn't have to go through this phase with him; they part
- some time after, Kathy learns that Tommy has "completed"
- she stops at a field in Norfolk where, she imagines, "everything I'd ever lost since my childhood had washed up"; fantasises Tommy appearing across the field on the horizon
- she cries and drives off "to wherever it was I was supposed to be"

Places and Events in *Never Let Me Go*

	Part One (1–9)	Part Two (10–17)	Part Three (18–23)
Places	childhood until 13: **golden age** 14 to 16: **darker years** students leave at 16	for two years veterans from other institutions	donors – carers
	Hailsham	**The Cottages**	**Dover, Norfolk**
Decisive Events	Miss Lucy's hints *(Ch. 3)*	theory of possibles *(Ch. 12)*	trip to stranded boat *(Ch. 19)*
	Madame's visits *(Ch. 3)*	trip to Norfolk *(Ch. 13-15)*	Kathy and Tommy – a couple *(Ch. 20)*
	Kathy's dance *(Ch. 6)*	Tommy's gallery theory *(Ch. 15)*	Kathy and Tommy at Madame's *(Ch. 21)*
	Madame's reaction *(Ch. 6)*		

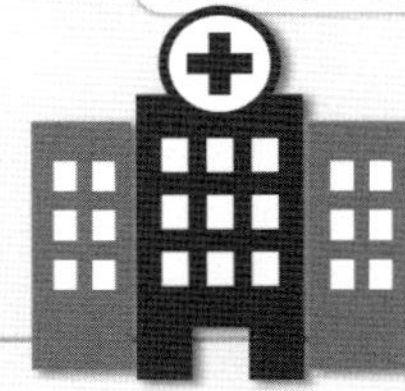

3 Characters

"Ordinary" humans/non-clones

Miss Emily

- Miss Emily is the **head guardian** at Hailsham.
- She is part of a movement to prove that clones have souls and wants them to be **treated more humanely**.
- In order to allow her students a carefree childhood, she **does not tell them the whole truth** about the donation programme.
- The students are **scared of her** (as she seems to know everything), but also consider her to be **fair** and respect her decisions; her presence makes them feel safe.

Madame (Marie-Claude)

- Like Miss Emily, Madame advocates for a **better treatment of clones**.
- She only visits Hailsham from time to time to **collect the students' artwork**.
- When meeting the clones, she seems shy and afraid, but also **feels sorry** for their fate.

Miss Lucy (Lucy Wainright)

- Miss Lucy is **popular** with the students, an excellent guardian and very **idealistic**.
- She believes the students should be made **more aware** of what lies ahead of them and **hints at their future usage**.
- Ultimately, she has to leave Hailsham because she does not follow Miss Emily's rules (not to tell the clones the truth).

Minor characters

- **Miss Geraldine:** students' favourite guardian; gentle, soft-spoken, always comforting them
- **Keffers:** ill-tempered caretaker at the Cottages

Clones

Kathy H.

- Kathy is the **first-person narrator** of the novel and tells the story by jumping back and forth in time.
- She is 31 years old and an **efficient carer**.
- Compared to her friend Ruth, she is more reserved and introverted.
- She has been in an **emotional triangle** with Ruth and Tommy since her youth (strong connection with Tommy; ups and downs in her friendship with Ruth).
- As an adult, Kathy becomes Ruth's carer; after Ruth's death, she first becomes Tommy's carer, then his lover.

Ruth

- Ruth appears **manipulative** and **commanding** at times (e. g. she is the undisputed leader of the "secret guard").
- She does not lie, but often denies certain things and implies others.
- During most of her time at Hailsham and the Cottages, she is in a **relationship with Tommy**.
- She is **best friends with Kathy**, but also **jealous** of Kathy's emotional connection with Tommy and tries to keep the two apart (although she knows that they would fit together perfectly).
- She asks Kathy for forgiveness in the end and they reconcile.

Tommy D.

- As a young student at Hailsham, Tommy is a **social outsider** and mocked for his fits of anger and lack of creativity.
- He is **torn between Ruth and Kathy** and becomes first Ruth's, then Kathy's lover.
- As an adult, he makes lots of drawings (of fantastic animals) in order to be granted deferral.

Minor characters

- **Chrissie and Rodney:** veteran couple at the Cottages; initiate search for Ruth's possible in Norfolk

4 Themes and interpretation

The themes dealt with in *Never Let Me Go* relate to the major topics "visions of the future", "dystopian literature" and "ethics of science".

Visions of the future

People are curious by nature and want to know what life has in store for them. Scientists are well aware of the enormous difficulties of predicting the future, but writers and filmmakers are free to **speculate and develop visions of their own**. Basically, one can differentiate between two kinds of literary visions of the future: **utopias** (positive representations), and **dystopias** (negative, nightmarish visions).

Background information

16th century	– In 1561, Sir Thomas More (1478–1535) published a political essay entitled *Utopia*. In it, he described an ideal place of harmony, tolerance and equality. Since then, the term "**utopia**" has become synonymous with positive visions of the future.
19th and early 20th century	– Inspired by the use of machinery during the Industrial Revolution, authors increasingly included **technical and scientific innovations** in their writings. – Early writers of literary visions of the future (such as H. G. Wells and Jules Verne) were by and large **optimistic** about the effects of technical achievements and developments. Similarly, American science fiction writers such as Isaac Asimov and Arthur C. Clarke believed in progress and the **blessings of technology**.
20th and early 21st century	– The First World War, the rise of the Communist regime in Russia and the Nazi regime in Germany **changed the optimistic mood** and authors expressed their fears for the future of mankind in **dystopias**. – Since the 1970s dystopian novels have outnumbered positive utopian visions of the future.

depiction in the novel

- *Never Let Me Go* is not really a vision of the future, but rather an example of "**alternate history**" → the action is set in the late 1990s, well before the novel was published (2005)

- Ishiguro wants the reader to realise that the phenomena he writes about are already present in our society today → makes his observations even more frightening

Dystopian literature

In contrast to a **utopia** (or positive vision of the future), the term **dystopia** is used to describe a highly negative representation of the future. Writers of dystopian literature often criticise existing social or technological developments by exaggerating them and showing where they might lead in the long run.

Background information

classic examples of dystopian literature and their main topics	**biotechnology** – Aldous Huxley, ***Brave New World*** (1932): state controls people by means of science (e. g. genetic engineering, drug "soma" to make people feel happy); knowing the truth vs. blissful ignorance **surveillance and the suppression of individual and minority interests** – George Orwell, ***Nineteen Eighty-Four*** (1949): state controls people by means of constant surveillance and propagandistic language ("Newspeak") – Ray Bradbury, ***Fahrenheit 451*** (1953): state bans books and replaces them with superficial entertainment (to stop people from thinking critically) – Margaret Atwood, ***The Handmaid's Tale*** (1985): theocratic state completely suppresses women – Suzanne Collins, ***The Hunger Games*** (2008 – 2010): state uses a perverse game show (in which the candidates have to fight for their survival) to keep citizens in check; two-class society (rich Capitol vs. poor districts) – Dave Eggers, ***The Circle*** (2013): social networking sites dominate people's lives; total transparency replaces total surveillance (reversal of Orwell's *Nineteen Eighty-Four*) **end-of-the-world scenarios (apocalypses)** – Edan Lepucki, ***California*** (2014), Nevil Shute, ***On the Beach*** (1947) and Cormac McCarthy, ***The Road*** (2006): ecological or nuclear catastrophes lead to a complete breakdown of human society; struggle for survival – Kurt Vonnegut, "**Tomorrow and Tomorrow and Tomorrow**" (1953) and J. G. Ballard, "**Billennium**" (1961): overpopulation leads to dreadful living conditions

depiction in the novel

Kazuo Ishiguro's novel contains several dystopian elements. He paints a sombre picture of a society which has become deeply inhumane:

- the state has established a national programme to "produce" organs → creation of a **two-class society** divided into "ordinary" humans and clones (who are regarded as mere stock of spare parts)
- the clones exist in a sort of **parallel world** (institutions like Hailsham, the Cottages, various recovery centres); little contact with non-clones
- the clones' futures are **predetermined** → helplessness (see e. g. Tommy's cry after he has learnt the truth about the programme)
- the clones ultimately comply with their fate → **no resistance** against the system
- theme of **knowledge vs. ignorance:**
  students at Hailsham are not told (or are too young to understand) the whole truth about donations (Miss Emily's intention to "protect" the clones vs. Miss Lucy's attempts to be more open) → lack of information leads to **rumours and speculations** (e. g. about deferrals); most non-clones do not want to know where organs come from and prefer blissful ignorance → **lack of empathy**
- **language as ideological tool** to cover up the cruelty of the programme (e. g. "to complete" as euphemism for "to die"; term "donor" suggests voluntariness)

Ethics of science

With new scientific advances in the spheres of **biotechnology** (such as genome editing), the questions "How far can scientists go? Should man be allowed to play God?" have become ever more pressing. Are scientists free to research without any restrictions and **implement any kind of new technology**, or do we have to **impose limitations** based on generally agreed morals and social values?

Background information

examples of biotechnology in medicine	**genome editing** – definition: making specific changes to the DNA of an organism by means of gene "scissors" – defective cells can be corrected; when this is done in body cells, the changes are not passed on to children – changes to sperms or egg cells are passed on to future generations; can lead to the creation of enhanced humans **therapeutic cloning** – definition: using stem cells from a cloned embryo to create tissues or cells that are genetically identical to those of a patient – it is possible to cure diseases and extend life by replacing defective cells or organs, no need for human organ donors – but: embryos destroyed to gain stem cells **reproductive cloning** – definition: creating a genetic copy of a whole individual – so far prohibited for humans (raises profound ethical problems)

depiction in the novel

Never Let Me Go deals with the **reproductive cloning of humans**. The main protagonists are genetic copies of "ordinary" humans, raised for the sole purpose of providing organs for transplant. Ishiguro does not expand on the technical or scientific aspect of cloning, but rather warns of its **moral implications:**

- **the clones are regarded as less than human:**
  - society wants to see clones as soulless beings in order to justify the use of organs
  - however, throughout the novel, the clones are presented as **multi-layered individuals with strong emotions** (see e. g. the complex emotional relationship between Kathy, Ruth and Tommy; the clones' hopes and dreams for the future; Ruth's disappointment that she did not find her possible; Tommy's desperation after finding out that there are no deferrals, etc.)
- **the clones are instrumentalised:** the clones are not valued in themselves, but are degraded to a mere means to an end (supply organs for other people)

- **the clones are not given the right to self-determination:** they are not allowed to take free decisions; their futures are already set out for them and determined by their purpose; for instance, they must lead a healthy lifestyle (Miss Emily's warning not to smoke); they cannot pursue a profession (except as "carers"); as young adults they will inevitably become donors until they die
- **cloning challenges conventional social relationships (between relatives or generations):** the clones grow up without parents or relatives; they are fascinated with the question of who their possible might be and how old that person might be (their parents' age or almost the same age?)
- **scientists create "superclones":** Morningdale scandal: a scientist has already created clones with enhanced genetic characteristics → leads to eugenics

"Two Kinds" and "The Child"

1 "Two Kinds"

1.1 Key facts about the short story

- **author:** Amy Tan (*1952 in Oakland, California), parents immigrated to the United States from China (Shanghai) in 1948
- **year of publication:** 1989; contained in Tan's first book *The Joy Luck Club* (a novel about a club founded in San Francisco by four Chinese immigrant women and their four American-born daughters, who tell each other stories)
- **genre:** short story
- **narrative perspective:** first-person narration; as an adult, the narrator looks back on occurrences during her childhood
- **content:** Jing-Mei, a young Chinese girl, rebels against her ambitious mother's plans to make her a star.
- **explanation of title:** According to Jing-Mei's mother, there are only two kinds of daughters: "Those who are obedient and those who follow their own mind!"

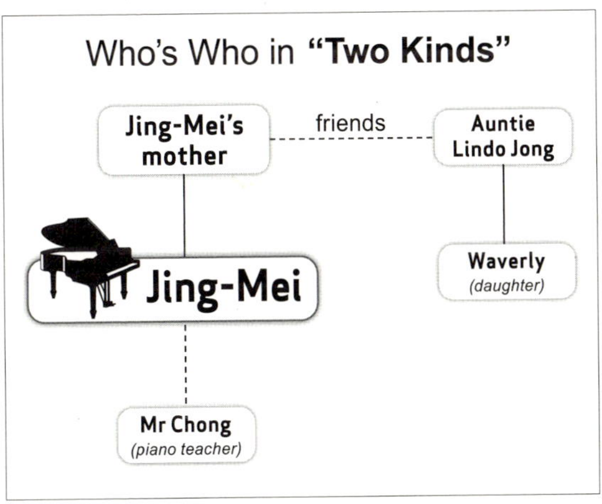

1.2 Plot

- Jing-Mei's mother wants her nine-year-old daughter to be a prodigy
- first try: Jing-Mei supposed to become a child actress, singer and dancer (like Shirley Temple) → Jing-Mei cooperates because she wants to be famous herself, but plan does not work out
- next: mother looks for stories about talented children in magazines → tests Jing-Mei every day (e. g. multiplying numbers in head)
- Jing-Mei begins to hate the tests → finally, mother gives up hope and stops testing her daughter
- a few months later: new idea (inspired by TV show) → mother organises piano lessons for Jing-Mei
- piano teacher is deaf and incompetent
- Jing-Mei does not apply herself, determined not to try, practises in her own way (one year long)
- mother is proud and shows off to a friend about her daughter
- parents buy second-hand piano
- Jing-Mei supposed to perform in public at a talent show → very confident to do well
- performance ends in disaster, mother does not say a word
- two days later: mother expects Jing-Mei to practise the piano again → confrontation escalates
- from then on: no piano lessons anymore, strained mother-daughter relationship
- on 30th birthday: mother offers piano as a present, Jing-Mei refuses
- after mother's death: Jing-Mei plays the piano again for the first time after many years → sentimental feelings

1.3 Characters

Jing-Mei (narrator)

- At first, Jing-Mei is an **obedient child** and follows her mother's instructions since she **wants to be famous** herself.
- Over the course of time, however, her mother's ambitions put her **under too much pressure**.

- She becomes aware of her deficiencies, finds her mother's expectations are unrealistic and **rebels** against her.
- As an adult, she is **more tolerant** and shows **greater understanding** for her mother's intentions.

Jing-Mei's mother

- Jing-Mei's mother **emigrated from China** in 1949, leaving behind her parents, first husband and losing her twin daughters.
- She firmly **believes in the American Dream** and is convinced that America offers almost unlimited opportunities.
- She is **very ambitious** for her daughter and tries everything to make Jing-Mei succeed in society.
- Her style of parenting is **very strict:** she expects her daughter to be obedient and is ready to use violence if necessary (slaps Jing-Mei or drags her by the arm).
- She competes with her friend Lindo Jong, whose daughter is very successful in playing chess.
- She is very **hardworking** and ready to make sacrifices for her daughter's success (house cleaning services in exchange for piano lessons).
- A big row with Jing-Mei seems to bring an end to her dreams, leaving her **disappointed**.
- However, she appears to believe in her daughter's talent until the end and to have mellowed over time (offers Jing-Mei the piano as a present).

Minor characters

- **Auntie Lindo Jong:** a friend of Jing-Mei's mother; brags about her chess-playing daughter Waverly ("Chinatown's Littlest Chinese Chess Champion")
- **Mr Chong:** retired piano teacher; kind and friendly, but incompetent and deaf; nicknamed Old Chong by Jing-Mei; not married, lives with his mother

2 "The Child"

2.1 Key facts about the short story

- **author:** Julius Lester (1939–2018), politically active in Civil Rights Movement, university professor
- **year of publication:** first version in 1960 (while fight for racial equality was in full swing), revised in 1993 for collection *Join In: Multiethnic Short Stories by Outstanding Writers for Young Adults*
- **genre:** short story
- **narrative perspective:** third-person limited narration
- **content:** During a ride on the subway, Karen, a pregnant African American teenage girl, thinks about her past, present and future.
- **explanation of title:** "The Child" can refer to both Karen, who is still quite young, and the baby in her womb.

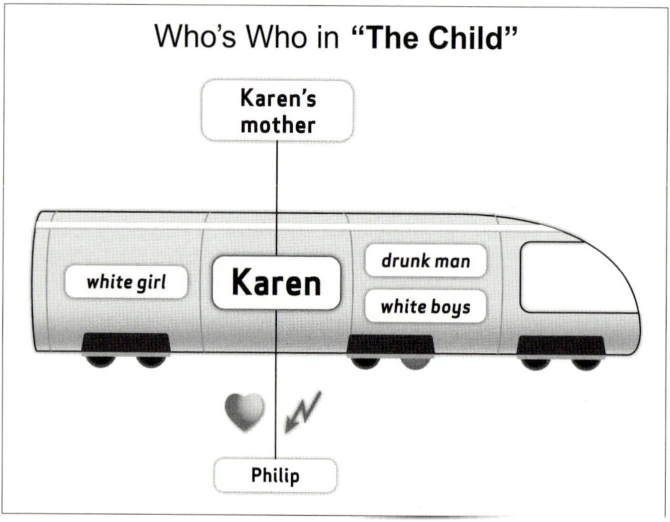

2.2 Plot

- 17-year-old Karen goes down to the subway and waits on the platform
- nobody pays attention to her
- a black, drunk man swears all the time → makes Karen feel sorry for him as well as ashamed of being black herself
- she thinks about the argument she had with her mother because of her unplanned pregnancy: mother was so furious that she slapped Karen, Karen slapped back
- people board the subway, no one offers Karen a seat
- Karen remembers meeting Philip: she was happy and in love, but then Philip disappointed her (refused to support her with the baby)
- she notices a white girl, who is reading a book → admires and envies her, is curious about the girl's dreams
- Karen tries to be optimistic (finish school after having baby) although her friends' experience shows the opposite; imagines a prosperous future for her child
- at the next station: a group of white boys take the few empty seats
- the boys make fun of the drunk man
- Karen makes promises to her unborn baby: she will finish school, become a successful fashion designer and they will have a good life
- she hides her tears

2.3 Characters

Karen

- Karen is a **pregnant 17-year-old black student**.
- She is small, younger looking, plain and **not very self-confident**.
- She has sweet memories of her first love experience: when she met Philip, she felt pretty and seen for the first time in her life.
- Although the pregnancy was not planned and she is going to be a single mother, she is **proud to be pregnant** and already thinks like a caring mother.
- Nevertheless, she is **insecure about her own future**.

Karen’s mother

- Karen’s mother is **ambitious** for her daughter.
- She is a **hardworking** woman, making sacrifices (two jobs) to pay for Karen’s education and training.
- She is **religious** and believes Karen’s pregnancy would have been prevented if Karen had been a faithful Christian.
- Because of Karen’s untimely pregnancy her dream is shattered, leaving her **frustrated**.

Minor characters

- **Philipp:** irresponsible youth; had sex with Karen and left her when she got pregnant
- **white girl on the train:** seems self-assured in Karen’s view, not a care in the world; symbolises Karen’s own unattainable dream
- **drunk man:** dirty face and clothes; frustrated, angry; in Karen’s view a disgrace to black people
- **white boys:** loud and rowdy; make fun of the drunk man

3 Themes and interpretation

The themes dealt with in the two short stories relate to the major topics "(ethnic) identity", "growing up" and "The American Dream".

Ethnic identity

An individual's ethnic identity can refer to his or her **membership in a cultural or social group**. Generally speaking, people tend to assume the ethnic identity of their parents – or at least one parent. **Problems** can arise, especially for young people, when they grow up in a society in which the ethnic group of their parents represents a **minority** and/ or when they feel **torn between two cultures**.

Ethnic identity in "Two Kinds"

- family background: Jing-Mei grows up in two different cultures, Chinese and American
- at home Jing-Mei is taught to obey her parents and apply herself in order to succeed
- outside home Jing-Mei experiences American lifestyle and values
- Jing-Mei wants more freedom and self-determination
- different views result in clash with her mother

Ethnic identity in "The Child"

- family background: Karen grows up in an African American family
- drunk black man makes her feel ashamed of her race
- conscious of belonging to a disadvantaged ethnic minority; perceives racial discrimination/inequality: white unruly boys get away with their rowdy behaviour; she envies the white girl who seems "to be free of other people's thoughts and opinions and ideas about [her]"

Growing up

During adolescence, young people mature and begin to develop relationships and explore their own identity. The **search for independence in thinking and behaviour** can be accompanied by problems such as identity crises, self-doubts, low self-esteem, disappointments, disillusions and conflicts – often between adolescents and their parents.

Growing up in "Two Kinds"

- Jing-Mei's self-esteem decreases more and more every time she has to disappoint her mother ("I looked in the mirror [...] and I saw only my face staring back and understood that it would always be this ordinary face. I began to cry. Such a sad, ugly girl!")
- Jing-Mei realises that she is unable to live up to her mother's expectations → decides to stop being obedient ("I won't let her change me, I promised myself. I won't be what I'm not.") → rebels to achieve independence and self-determination
- escalation of mother-daughter conflict: mother uses violence, daughter offends mothe[illegible]sh I were dead! Like them." – referring to the tw[illegible]other had lost)
- names of piano pieces symbolise Jing-Mei's process of maturing: through childhood, she is the "Pleading Child", wanting her mother's attention and praise ↔ as an adult, she is "Perfectly Contented", knowing who she is

Growing up in "The Child"

- Karen's self-perception: feels inferior, unloved and neglected ("She had lived for seventeen years, and no one had noticed.")
- search for acceptance and affection might have made her fall for Philip
- being pregnant at 17, Karen is forced to grow up faster than others
- escalation of mother-daughter conflict: Karen retaliates against her mother's reproach ("How could you let something like this happen?") by telling her she made the same mistake at 17; they slap each other

The American Dream

The idea of the American Dream is the **hope for a better future for anybody who is willing to work hard**. This concept ("from rags to riches" or "from dishwasher to millionaire") has also been a **major driving force behind immigration** to the United States. In recent decades, however, criticism that the dream is no longer alive is growing louder. Ethnic minorities, in particular Native Americans and African Americans, feel they have been denied the promise of social mobility.

The American Dream in "Two Kinds"

- Jing-Mei's mother's dreams:
  - better life in America ("My mother believed you could be anything you wanted to be in America.") → reason for leaving China
  - Jing-Mei will be a star → wants her daughter to achieve what she was unable to attain herself, i. e. to live the American Dream

  After the disastrous performance at the recital and the ensuing struggle at the piano, Jing-Mei's mother seems to abandon her dreams ("The lid to the piano was closed, shutting out the dust, my misery, and her dreams.").
- Jing-Mei's dream: at first, she likes idea of being a child prodigy ↔ later, she only wants to be accepted the way she is: as an average person ("I could only be me.")

The American Dream in "The Child"

- Karen's mother's dream: Karen will be a famous fashion designer ("My daughter is going to be somebody!") → wants her daughter to achieve what she was unable to attain herself (because of her own pregnancy)
- Karen's pregnancy destroys her mother's dream
- at first, Karen likewise transfers her own dreams and ambitions to her unborn baby ("Seventeen years from next spring, her baby would finish school for both of them.") – like her mother did when she had Karen at 17
- however, Karen realises that she shouldn't have dreams for her child
- she thinks that only white people can dream ("it didn't pay to be black and to dream")
- hopes to finish school and become a famous fashion designer in spite of unplanned pregnancy, but also realises that her future is uncertain → starts crying

Dreams in …

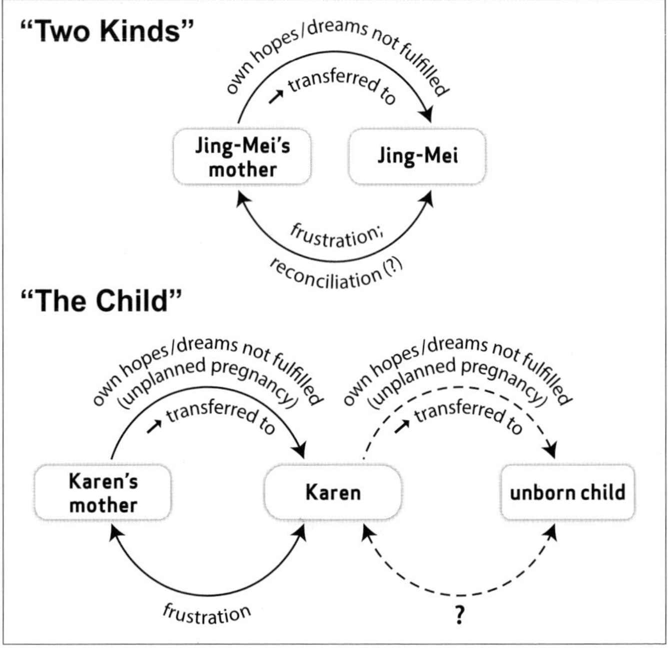
"Two Kinds"
own hopes/dreams not fulfilled
transferred to
Jing-Mei's mother
Jing-Mei
frustration;
reconciliation (?)
"The Child"
own hopes/dreams not fulfilled (unplanned pregnancy)
transferred to
own hopes/dreams not fulfilled (unplanned pregnancy)
transferred to
Karen's mother
Karen
unborn child
frustration
?

Crash

1 Key facts about the film

- **screenplay:** written by Paul Haggis (*1953 in London, Ontario, Canada) and Bobby Moresco (*1951 in New York City, USA), real-life inspiration (Haggis first conceived the project after he was car-jacked at gunpoint in 1991)
- **director and producer:** Paul Haggis
- **release date:** 2004
- **awards:** Oscar for Best Picture and for Best Original Screenplay (both in 2005)
- **genre:** drama
- **running time:** ca. 108 minutes
- **structure:** a so-called **episodic film** (narrates events in people's lives during two days: the events run parallel up to the point of collision, but the film tells the stories moving back and forth from one perspective to another, thus illustrating how intertwined and connected their relations in reality are), unchronological presentation of events (beginning – flashback – end)
- **setting:** Los Angeles, California
- **content:** The characters in the film all live in the same city, but come from different ethnic and social backgrounds. As a result, they lead relatively separate lives and do not have any contact with each other – at first. However, their paths cross unexpectedly, and these random encounters reveal deep-rooted social issues (such as racial prejudices) which are normally hidden under the surface.

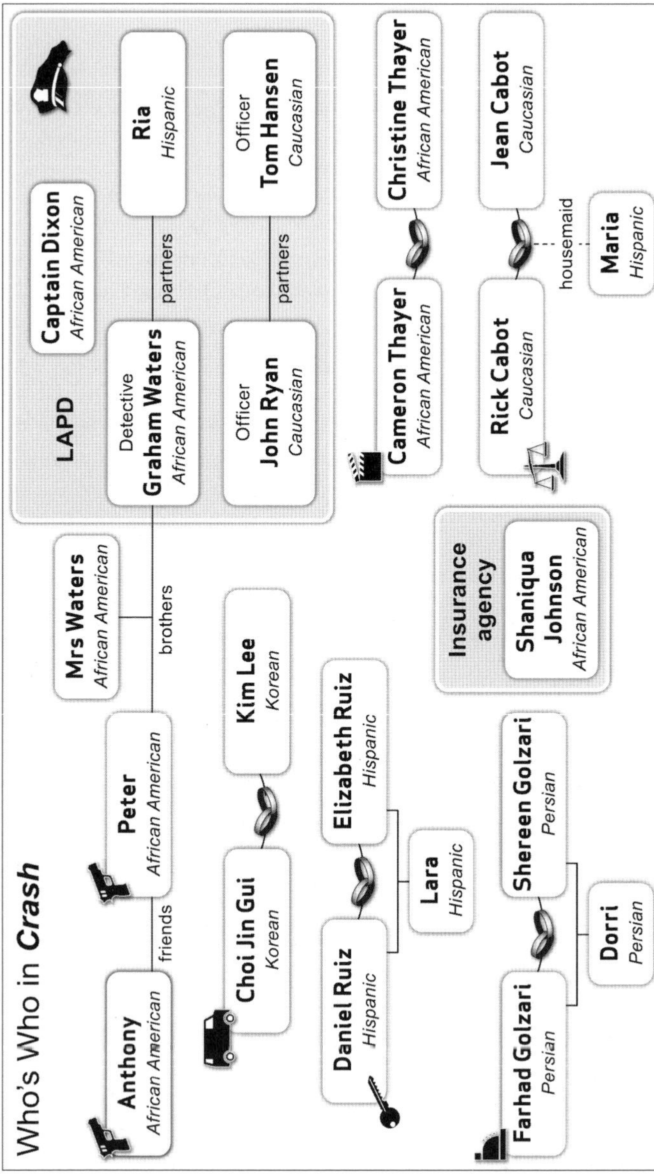
Who's Who in Crash
LAPD
Captain Dixon
African American
Detective
Graham Waters
African American
partners
Ria
Hispanic
Officer
John Ryan
Caucasian
partners
Officer
Tom Hansen
Caucasian
Mrs Waters
African American
brothers
Anthony
African American
friends
Peter
African American
Choi Jin Gui
Korean
Kim Lee
Korean
Daniel Ruiz
Hispanic
Lara
Hispanic
Elizabeth Ruiz
Hispanic
Cameron Thayer
African American
Christine Thayer
African American
Rick Cabot
Caucasian
Jean Cabot
Caucasian
housemaid
Maria
Hispanic
Insurance agency
Shaniqua Johnson
African American
Farhad Golzari
Persian
Dorri
Persian
Shereen Golzari
Persian

2 Plot

In order to give a clearer overview, the plot is presented according to the main characters involved.

Graham Waters and Ria

- on the way to a crime scene: collision with a woman (Kim Lee) → fierce argument between the two women (accusations, racist insults)
- Detective Waters arrives at crime scene: dead body discovered by the roadside

In a flashback, the film reveals the events of the last 36 hours up to the discovery of the corpse:

- Waters' family background: cares for his drug-addicted mother, who worries about her younger son Peter (who is always in trouble with the police)
- Waters and Ria are called to a crime scene which involves a shoot-out between two undercover police officers
- a man working for the district attorney asks Waters to cover up what happened (reason: the incident could damage the image and reputation of the police force)
- in return, promise to spare his brother Peter from imprisonment
- Waters reluctantly agrees to the deal
- in the end, his efforts are in vain: the dead body by the roadside turns out to be his brother Peter

Peter and Anthony

- Peter and Anthony carjack District Attorney Rick Cabot and his wife Jean
- Peter and Anthony drive through the city in the stolen black SUV and run over a Korean man (Choi Jin Gui)
- they drop the injured person in front of the emergency entrance of a hospital
- they cannot sell the vehicle because of the blood stains inside
- Peter and Anthony try to carjack Cameron Thayer, who resists → Peter escapes, Anthony and Cameron are chased by the police
- later, Anthony steals the van of the man they ran over

- the van is packed with illegal Asian migrants → Korean man exposed as a people trafficker
- Anthony refuses an offer to sell these refugees, but releases them at a busy intersection in Chinatown
- the same night, Peter is given a lift by LAPD (Los Angeles Police Department) officer Tom Hansen, who is off duty → he is shot by Hansen due to a misunderstanding

Rick and Jean Cabot

- after the violent attack and the car theft, Jean Cabot has the locks changed in her home by the locksmith Daniel
- Jean wants to have the locks changed again in the morning (she does not trust Daniel)
- District Attorney Rick Cabot fears the car incident and news of a shooting between two undercover police agents could have a negative impact on his career and election prospects
- Rick and his staff put Detective Waters (who is investigating the case) under pressure to cooperate and falsify the facts

John Ryan

- LAPD officer Ryan is worried about his sick father
- he is angry and frustrated, because the health insurance company, represented by administrator Shaniqua Johnson, refuses to provide more effective treatment
- on night duty with his younger partner Tom Hansen, Ryan stops a black limousine which he takes for the Cabots' stolen SUV
- brushing aside Hansen's protest, he carries out a sexist and humiliating body search of the wife of the driver (Christine Thayer)
- later, Ryan saves the same woman's life, rescuing her from her burning car

Tom Hansen

- on night duty, Hansen and his partner Ryan stop a black limousine → Hansen watches his partner molesting Christine Thayer
- disgusted by his partner's racist behaviour, Hansen asks his boss, Captain Dixon, to be assigned a new partner → he has to go on duty in a one-man car

- he helps Cameron Thayer get out of a dangerous confrontation with the police (after a car chase)
- driving home at night, he gives Peter (who is standing by the roadside) a lift, they have a friendly chat
- when Peter reaches into his pocket to show Tom his Christopher figure, the officer wrongly assumes the boy is about to pull a gun → he panics and shoots Peter, acting, as he thinks, in self-defence
- to get rid of the dead body, Hansen stops, dumps the corpse in a field and sets the car on fire

Cameron and Christine Thayer

- following the degrading body search by John Ryan, the couple argue: Christine complains about her husband's weak resistance and lack of support during the police control, Cameron accuses his wife of unrealistic ideas about what it is like to be black → the argument causes a deep split in their relationship
- Christine gets into a car accident and is rescued by John Ryan
- Cameron becomes the victim of an unsuccessful carjacking incident (by Peter and Anthony) and almost gets shot by LAPD officers after a car chase
- in the end the couple reconcile

Farhad and Dorri Golzari

- with the help of his daughter Dorri, Farhad Golzari buys himself a weapon and ammunition, because he fears for his family's safety after his wife has been attacked
- one of the shop doors does not close properly → Farhad wants the lock to be repaired ↔ locksmith Daniel changes the lock and warns Farhad: bent door is the more serious problem, he should have it replaced → Farhad feels exploited, refuses to pay the bill
- shop is broken into → Farhad feels cheated, holds Daniel responsible
- armed with his gun, he ambushes the locksmith → shoots at Daniel but, by accident, hits his daughter Lara
- luckily, Lara is not hurt (as the gun is loaded with blanks instead of live bullets, which Farhad does not know) → the completely shocked Farhad hands the gun to his daughter Dorri

Daniel and Lara Ruiz

- the locksmith has moved into a new, more secure neighbourhood, because his young daughter Lara had become so scared of shootings in the area where the family first lived
- to further convince Lara that she is now safe, Daniel pretends to cover her with an invisible and impenetrable cloak
- Daniel changes the locks at the Cabots' house and hears Jean Cabot making disparaging remarks about him
- he also changes the lock at Farhad Golzari's shop and is insulted when he advises the shopkeeper to have the whole door replaced
- when Daniel is held at gunpoint by angry Farhad Golzari, the situation between them escalates
- Lara decides to jump into her father's arms so that she can protect him with her invisible cloak → when Farhad shoots, Lara is hit
- Lara escapes attack unhurt → she believes the magic cloak protected her

3 Characters

Detective Graham Waters

- The **detective** is in his thirties, a chain smoker, rather **quiet and reserved**.
- He has two worries: his drug addicted mother and his younger brother Peter, who often gets into trouble with the law.
- Initially, Waters gives the impression that he has everything under control, but his **self-assurance disappears** when he has to agree to a deal which he knows is not right.

Officer John Ryan

- Having served in the LAPD for seventeen years, John Ryan is an **experienced police officer** who has "seen it all".
- His superior and his colleagues know about his **racist attitudes**, his outspoken, ruthless and rough manner, but respect him for his **proficiency**.

- Although he harasses and humiliates Christine Thayer, he helps her escape from her burning car without thinking twice about his own safety.
- The stress and frustration which he experiences in his private life – he cannot get better health care for his father, who is in great pain – adds to his anger and has an impact on his work as a police officer.

Officer Tom Hansen

- The **young inexperienced police officer** starts his career in the LAPD as John Ryan's partner.
- He is disgusted by Ryan's unjustified body search of Christine Thayer, because this behaviour is in stark contrast to his belief that everybody should be treated with **respect and fairness**.
- However, in the end, he is shocked by the sobering realisation that he himself is **racially prejudiced** and that his own **idealist views** do not stand the test of reality.

Rick Cabot

- The District Attorney is a **smart**, **career-minded politician**, an **opportunist**, who is set on increasing his influence and status by all means, such as **manipulating** the press and the electorate to create a positive image.
- He stays in the background to keep his hands clean and uses his staff (Karen and Flanagan) for unlawful manoeuvres.

Jean Cabot

- The **haughty**, **bored and frustrated housewife** living a life of **luxury** feels neglected and suspects her husband of having an affair with his assistant Karen.
- She feels sorry for herself and takes her anger out on her home help Maria and the locksmith Daniel.

Farhad Golzari

- The shopkeeper **immigrated** to the US **from Iran**.
- As he **can barely speak and understand English**, he is unable to make himself understood.
- He **feels like an outsider**, cheated and mistreated as a terrorist.
- His anger erupts in a mad and almost fatal attack on Daniel Ruiz.
- Only when he realises what an atrocious act he has committed does he come to his senses again.

Daniel Ruiz

- The **locksmith** Daniel is in his twenties.
- Because of his appearance – close-cropped hair, baggy pants and tattoos – prejudiced Jean Cabot and Farhad Golzari mistake him for a gangster and trickster.
- In reality, Daniel is not only a **hard worker**, but also a **loving and caring husband and father**.

Cameron and Christine Thayer

- The Thayers are a **black couple** of the well-to-do **upper middle class**.
- Cameron, in his forties, is a **successful TV director**; his beautiful, **light-skinned wife** is a woman who knows what she wants.
- Racial prejudice and discrimination nearly ruin their harmonious relationship.
- Christine tries hard to make up for her brusque and unfair accusations against her husband.

Anthony and Peter

- Peter (Graham Waters' younger brother) is the quieter, more reserved and less daring of these **two criminals**.
- Anthony is loudmouthed, constantly rambling on about racial discrimination, even when it sounds ridiculous (e. g. when he refers to hip-hop music as an invention of white people to suppress African Americans).

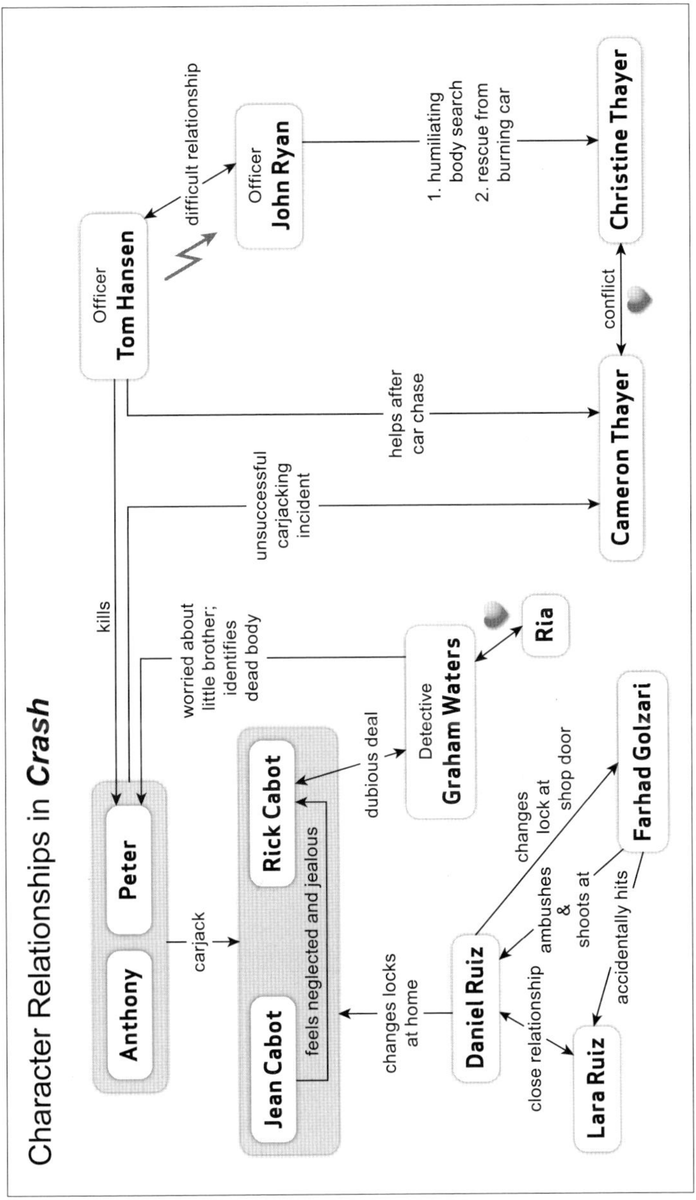

Character Relationships in *Crash*

4 Themes and interpretation

The themes dealt with in *Crash* relate to the major topics "ethnic and cultural diversity" and "beliefs, values and norms in society".

Stereotyping, racial prejudice and discrimination

The traditional and cherished **ideal of American society as a melting pot** in which various racial and ethnic groups are combined into one culture is disclosed as a **myth**. Racism is a widespread phenomenon in American society. Irrespective of their ethnic backgrounds, people are often **biased in their view of other ethnic groups** and consequently misled in their actions.

depiction in the film

- the huge metropolis L.A. is used as a model to show that people of diverse ethnic backgrounds have not assimilated into one society sharing a common cultural life and values → although they live in the same city, they have remained different and separate from each other
- all the characters in the movie jump to conclusions based on racial prejudice and fall into the trap of racism (e. g. when the gun seller treats Farhad Golzari like a terrorist, when Jean Cabot regards Daniel as a criminal due to his shaved head and tattoos or when Tom Hansen wrongly feels endangered by Peter and kills the innocent man)

Racism and police shootings

In numerous movies, novels and television shows the LAPD has been associated with **police brutality**, **corruption** and **racial profiling** – deservedly or not. In recent years, there have generally been more complaints about **arbitrary police controls** ("stop and search") against African Americans, especially black youths. Statistics prove that US police shoot disproportionally more black than white civilians, even when these people are unarmed. Several incidents, such as the Michael Brown case of 2014, resulted in **violent clashes with the police and**

race riots, for example in L.A., New York, Ferguson, St. Louis and Baltimore. The nationwide debate about racism in law enforcement led to the foundation of the "Black Lives Matter" movement.

depiction in the film

- John Ryan is a racially biased LAPD officer, who carries out a humiliating body search on Christine Thayer, which he would hardly have done if Christine had been white

Affirmative action

The policy of affirmative action was one of the main achievements of the Civil Rights Movement of the 1960s. The programme was introduced to **protect marginalised groups** from being discriminated against, especially in employment. To improve the situation for these groups on the labour market, employers were required to select job applicants from ethnic minorities even if candidates from those groups had lower test scores than white applicants. Not long after the system had come into practice, white people complained about "**reverse discrimination**", arguing that merit should be the only criterion for a job and not race, sex or religion. The acceptance of the affirmative action policy has generally declined, and even members of marginalised groups, who were supposed to profit from affirmative action, are not all pleased about the practice.

depiction in the film

- John Ryan insults health insurance administrator Shaniqua Johnson, saying that she only got the job because she is black ("I can't look at you without thinking about the five or six more qualified white men that didn't get your job.")
- John Ryan is furious because the affirmative action policy destroyed his father's business ("He struggled his whole life. Saved enough to start his own company. 23 employees, all of them black. Paid them equal wages when no one else was doing that. […] Then the City Council gives minority owned companies preference. Overnight my father loses everything. His business, his home, his wife. And not once does he blame your people.")

Crime, violence and gun culture

The fact that the crime index in Los Angeles is higher than in other US cities has earned the city the epithet "**gang capital of the nation**". The number of car thefts at gunpoint features at the top of the list of violent offences. Criminologists regard car theft as a "debut crime" – a gateway to more serious offences. The term "**gun culture**" is used to describe the obsession of Americans with guns, which dates back to the days of the pioneers, who needed weapons for hunting and self-defence. The **Second Amendment** guarantees US citizens the right to "keep and bear arms", a constitutional right, which the influential National Rifle Association uses to prevent stricter gun laws ("Guns don't kill, people kill."). To reduce the crime rate two strategies were introduced: the policy of "**zero tolerance**" and the "**three-strikes law**". The courts did not accept any excuses, and offenders were severely punished. In addition, judges were required to impose harsher sentences on those who had been convicted of three or more serious criminal offences. In California, the application of the law has since been reduced as the prison population soared.

depiction in the film

- Anthony and Peter approach the car drivers Cabot and Thayer with a gun, threatening to shoot them if they do not turn over their cars
- the film includes numerous close-ups of handguns (in the gun shop, during Peter's and Anthony's "Saturday night specials", at the crime scene, in Farhad's shop)
- Peter finds himself confronted with the "three-strikes law"; only his brother's illegal cooperation saves him from imprisonment

Health insurance

Generally speaking, **medical service** is **extremely expensive** in the USA, and the high costs for proper health insurance have been **out of reach for lower income classes**, especially African Americans and unemployed people, for a long time. Millions have not had healthcare cover. Since the 1970s several Democratic presidents have tried to introduce basic health reforms in order to make healthcare affordable for uninsured Americans. Several attempts to improve health legislation failed, because Republicans adhered to their traditional view that everybody should care for themselves, and the state should not interfere. In 2010, President Barack Obama succeeded in getting a bill called the Patient Protection and Affordable Care Act (usually referred to as **Obamacare**) through Congress against the pressure of the opposition. It helps poorer Americans to pay for medicine and medical treatment.

depiction in the film

- John Ryan insults Shaniqua Johnson because he is frustrated about the refusal of the insurance company to pay for more expensive treatment for his father
- Shaniqua Johnson in turn argues that the healthcare plan that Ryan's father has is limited and does not cover extra costs

Hidden Figures

1 Key facts about the film

- **screenplay:** written by Theodore Melfi and Allison Schroeder, based on the non-fiction book *Hidden Figures: The American Dream and the Untold Story of the Black Women Who Helped Win the Space Race* by Margot Lee Shetterly (2016)
- **director:** Theodore Melfi (*1970 in New York City, USA)
- **release date:** 2016
- **awards:** nominated for three Oscars (Best Picture, Best Adapted Screenplay, Best Supporting Actress)
- **genre:** biographical drama
- **running time:** ca. 122 minutes
- **structure:** chronological presentation of events
- **setting:** White Sulphur Springs, West Virginia; Hampton, Virginia (particularly Langley Research Center)
- **time:** 1926; 1961/1962 (period of the Civil Rights Movement and the Space Race between the Soviet Union and the USA)
- **content:** Based on true events, the film tells the story of three African American women who work as mathematicians for the American space agency NASA. During a time of racial segregation and gender inequality, they are originally members of the "colored computers" until they are assigned to different departments. In their functions the three women contribute greatly to the successful launch of the spacecraft *Friendship 7* putting astronaut John Glenn as the first American into orbit around the Earth.

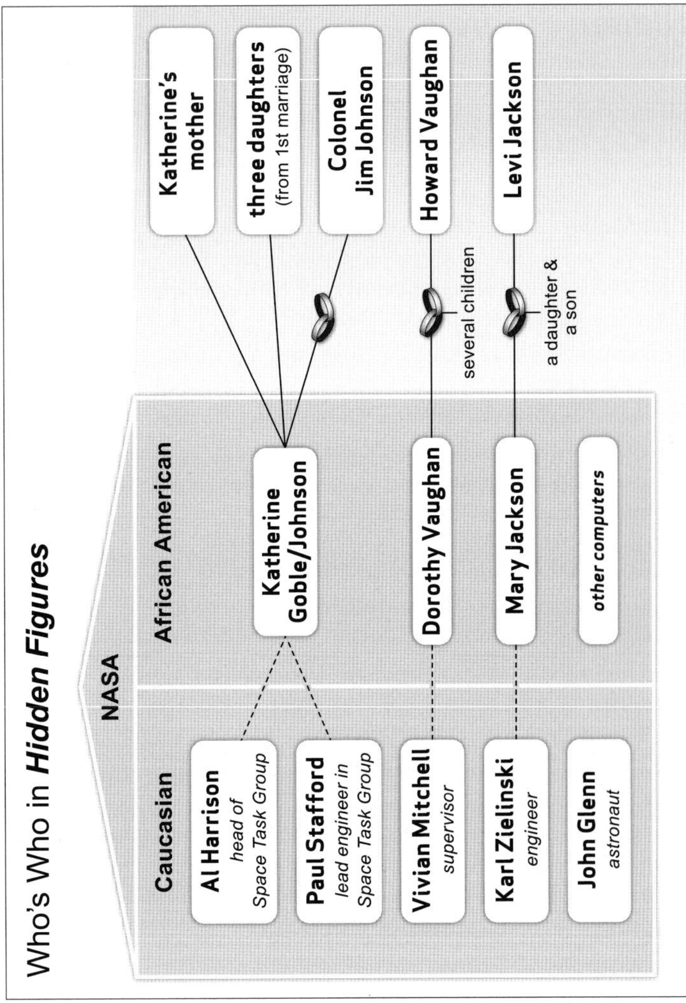
Who's Who in *Hidden Figures*
NASA
Caucasian
African American
Al Harrison
head of Space Task Group
Paul Stafford
lead engineer in Space Task Group
Vivian Mitchell
supervisor
Karl Zielinski
engineer
John Glenn
astronaut
Katherine Goble/Johnson
Dorothy Vaughan
Mary Jackson
other computers
Katherine's mother
three daughters
(from 1st marriage)
Colonel Jim Johnson
Howard Vaughan
several children
Levi Jackson
a daughter & a son

2 Plot

Background information	
Cold War	*Hidden Figures* is set against the backdrop of the Cold War, a period of **strong political tension** between the communist **Soviet Union** and the capitalist and democratic **USA**. It was feared that the conflict between the two superpowers could lead to a nuclear war.
Space Race	In the course of the Cold War, the USA and Russia competed in the spheres of science and space exploration, especially with regard to who would send the first person into space. The first human spaceflight programme by the US was called "**Project Mercury**"; the astronauts involved became known as the "**Mercury Seven**". Milestones of the Space Race mentioned in the film: – 9 March 1961: Russia puts spacecraft *Korabl-Sputnik 4* into low Earth orbit – 12 April 1961: Russia sends first human into orbit around the Earth (Yuri Gagarin, spacecraft: *Vostok*) – 5 May 1961: first American suborbital flight (Alan Shepard, *Mercury-Redstone 3/Freedom 7*) – 21 July 1961: second American suborbital flight (Gus Grissom, *Mercury-Redstone 4/Liberty Bell 7*) – 20 February 1962: first American orbital flight (John Glenn, *Mercury-Atlas 6/Friendship 7*)
computers	In the 1960s, the term "computers" still referred to **human computers** – i. e., to people carrying out complex mathematical calculations. The **West Computing Group** mentioned in the film were a group of African American women working at the NASA's Langley Research Center. The film also addresses the increasing automation due to the introduction of the **IBM machine**.

Setting 1 **White Sulphur Springs, West Virginia 1926 (ca. 00:39–02:58)** [1]

- 8-year old Katherine, a mathematics prodigy, receives a scholarship for a school where her talent can be furthered
- she solves an equation in front of her new class (all older than her)

Setting 2 **Hampton, Virginia 1961 (ca. 02:59–06:50)**

- Katherine Goble, Mary Jackson and Dorothy Vaughan are on their way to work: car has broken down → Dorothy manages to repair it
- white police officer escorts them to their workplace

1 Times refer to the DVD version of *Hidden Figures* and may vary slightly when played on different devices.

Setting 3 **Langley Research Center (ca. 06:51–09:53)**

- Russia has successfully launched *Korabl-Sputnik 4* and established orbital entry → at NASA, Americans are worried about Russian satellite (spying, nuclear threat)
- increased pressure on Al Harrison, head of the Space Task Group (STG), to provide an immediate response

Setting 4 **West Computing Group building (ca. 09:54–12:19)**

- Dorothy gives out new assignments to the West Computing Group (team of African American women): Mary is permanently assigned to Mercury project (at engineer Zielinski's request)
- the STG urgently needs a computer who is good at analytic geometry → Dorothy suggests Katherine
- Dorothy learns from Mrs Mitchell that her application for the position as supervisor of the West Computing Group is rejected

Setting 5 **Engineering department (ca. 12:20–15:01)**

- space capsule fails wind tunnel test → Mary and engineers examine it → Mary makes a good suggestion for improvement
- Zielinski encourages Mary to join the engineer training programme, but she hesitates because she is a black woman

Setting 6 **STG office (ca. 15:02–26:11)**

- instructions for Katherine on how to dress and behave
- Katherine is first mistaken for a janitor and stared at by STG's all-white staff
- Harrison announces arrival of the Mercury Seven astronauts and stresses the importance of the mission
- Katherine cannot check Mr Stafford's calculations, because he blacked out some of the figures
- Katherine hurries to the "colored ladies room" on the other side of the campus, takes work with her
- when she returns, there is even more work waiting for her
- Katherine pours herself a cup of coffee → disapproving looks

Setting 7 | **On the way home/Katherine's house (ca. 26:12–31:43)**

- Dorothy complains that despite her hard and reliable work she does not get promoted
- Dorothy encourages Katherine to believe in her abilities
- Katherine tells her mother and three daughters about her new job
- children complain about their mother's long working hours

Setting 8 | **Church (ca. 31:44–36:54)**

- pastor praises Martin Luther King's success in fighting for racial equality
- Levi Jackson struggles with his wife Mary's efforts in pursuing a career as an engineer
- Katherine meets Colonel Jim Johnson → they flirt with each other
- Jim talks disrespectfully about Katherine's job → she puts him in his place

Setting 9 | **NASA grounds (ca. 36:55–38:50)**

- arrival of Mercury Seven astronauts
- John Glenn takes time to chat with Dorothy, Mary and Katherine

Setting 10 | **STG office (ca. 38:51–40:07)**

- a separate, small, empty coffee pot labelled "Colored" has been provided for Katherine
- Katherine manages to read blacked out text by holding the paper up to the light
- Katherine starts to solve an equation on a large blackboard

Setting 11 | **Tech wing/East Computing Room (ca. 40:08–41:55)**

- newly arrived IBM computer does not fit through the door → wall needs to be torn down
- Dorothy is curious about the new machine and asks Mrs Mitchell about it → learns that it can supposedly do calculations much faster than human computers can

Setting 12 | **STG office (ca. 41:56–45:12)**

- Katherine finishes calculation on board, then hurries to bathroom
- in Katherine's absence: colleagues marvel at her work

- after Katherine's return: Harrison wonders if she is a Russian spy because she knows classified data → Katherine explains how she was able to read blacked-out information → Harrison orders that Katherine get uncensored reports in the future

Setting 13 **"Colored only" recreation room (ca. 45:13–46:25)**

- Dorothy fears that all human computers will lose their jobs due to new IBM → only solution: learn to operate it
- Mary's application for the engineer training programme is rejected (not qualified enough)

Setting 14 **Dorothy's house (ca. 46:26–47:55)**

- Dorothy encourages Mary to apply for courses at segregated school (if necessary by petitioning the court) to gain required qualifications

Setting 15 **In town (ca. 47:56–49:56)**

- Dorothy wants to borrow a book from the public library (not available in the "colored" section) → thrown out by security guard
- on the bus: Dorothy reveals that she has taken a book about Fortran (a programming language) with her

Setting 16 **Dorothy's house (ca. 49:57–52:56)**

- birthday party of one of Dorothy's sons
- Jim Johnson apologises to Katherine → they make up
- radio news: Russian cosmonaut, Yuri Gagarin, is the first man in space (12 April 1961)

Setting 17 **Langley Research Center/court (ca. 52:57–58:59)**

- Al Harrison urges his team to work even harder and longer
- IBM is installed but does not work
- Mary gets court date to fight for admission to Hampton High School
- Dorothy pays secret visits to the new IBM → teaches herself how to programme it
- Dorothy fixes problem and gets IBM to work

Setting 18 **STG office / West Computing Group building (ca. 59:00 – 01:03:22)**

- in pouring rain, Katherine hurries to bathroom on West Campus
- Harrison wonders where she goes every day for 40 minutes → questions her in front of staff
- Katherine vents her anger about segregation and discrimination (bathroom, payment, coffee pot)
- Harrison removes "Colored" label from coffee pot and takes down "Colored ladies room" sign

Setting 19 **Katherine's house (ca. 01:03:23 – 01:04:21)**

- Jim visits Katherine, who has the flu → dinner with the family

Setting 20 **Cape Canaveral (ca. 01:04:22 – 01:07:39)**

- successful launch of Alan Shepard and *Freedom 7* (5 May 1961)

Setting 21 **Katherine's house (ca. 01:07:40 – 01:08:59)**

- Katherine and Jim kiss for the first time

Setting 22 **Mary's house / court (ca. 01:09:00 – 01:12:05)**

- TV news: four white men accused of throwing a firebomb into a bus in Alabama
- Mary convinces the judge to allow her to attend courses at segregated high school (only night classes)

Setting 23 **STG office (ca. 01:12:06 – 01:13:38)**

- Katherine writes report, puts her name on byline (next to Stafford's) → Stafford refuses to accept it
- Harrison grants Katherine permission to work on Glenn's trajectory

Setting 24 **Dorothy's house / senate / STG office (ca. 01:13:39 – 01:17:28)**

- TV news: second Project Mercury flight, astronaut Gus Grissom recovered, but capsule lost (21 July 1961)
- senate hearing: Harrison promises success of John Glenn's upcoming mission
- STG discuss problem (how to get Glenn's capsule back down from orbit), Katherine is very committed, asks for access to briefings

Setting 25 | **IBM room (ca. 01:17:29–01:18:14)**

- Dorothy's unofficial work on the IBM: gets computer to run a programme and produce meaningful results → engineers are surprised

Setting 26 | **STG office/hallway/briefing room (ca. 01:18:15–01:23:52)**

- Katherine works on launch projections, but the details of the mission are changing fast → calculations wrong by the time she is done with them
- Katherine again puts her name on the report → Stafford wants her to "fix it"
- Katherine is finally allowed to attend Pentagon briefing → does current calculations for Glenn's flight on board; Glenn and other present men are impressed

Setting 27 | **IBM room/STG office (ca. 01:23:53–01:27:02)**

- Harrison puts pressure on IBM group → more programmers needed
- Dorothy is temporarily requested to work with IBM, willing to accept reassignment only if rest of "colored computers" can join
- whole West Computing Group is reassigned to work with IBM
- Katherine still at work in the late evening

Setting 28 | **Mary's house/Hampton High School (ca. 01:27:03–01:29:03)**

- Mary starts night classes, her husband supports her
- teacher and classmates are surprised when she enters the classroom

Setting 29 | **STG office/ladies' toilet (ca. 01:29:04–01:32:24)**

- Katherine comes up with excellent solution for "Launch, Landing, and Go/No Go Analysis", leaves out her name on report this time
- Mrs Mitchell tries to assure Dorothy that she is unprejudiced

Setting 30 | **Katherine's house (ca. 01:32:25–01:35:00)**

- Jim proposes to Katherine, she says yes

Setting 31 | **NASA grounds/Harrison's office (ca. 01:35:01–01:37:46)**

- preparations for Glenn's space flight
- STG no longer needs Katherine because IBM can do the calculations → Harrison must dismiss her; pearl necklace as a present

Setting 32 **Church (ca. 01:37:47–01:38:14)**

- wedding preparations

Setting 33 **Cape Canaveral / Langley Research Center (ca. 01:38:15–01:46:20)**

- day of John Glenn's launch (20 February 1962)
- problem with IBM calculations: landing coordinates do not match those from the day before
- Glenn requests that Katherine check the numbers by hand → Harrison sends for her
- Katherine checks calculations at her old desk in "colored computers" room while Glenn is getting ready to board *Friendship 7*
- Harrison grants Katherine access to control room
- revised coordinates confirmed to Glenn by phone
- spacecraft *Friendship 7* launches

Setting 34 **"Colored computers"' room (ca. 01:46:21–01:47:39)**

- new assignment for Dorothy: a permanent team to feed the IBM is needed, Dorothy is appointed IBM Computing Lab Supervisor
- Mrs Mitchell addresses her as "Mrs Vaughan" for the first time

Setting 35 **NASA control room (01:47:40–01:54:07)**

- warning light: malfunction with spacecraft's heat shield
- solution found, mission successfully completed (also thanks to Katherine)
- Harrison congratulates Katherine

Setting 36 **Various places (01:54:08–01:56:03)**

The film ends with a prospect on the following events:

- *Friendship 7* mission turned tide in space race; first crewed Moon landing (1969)
- Mary Jackson became NASA's and America's first female African American aeronautical engineer
- Dorothy Vaughan became a Fortran specialist and NASA's first African American supervisor
- Katherine Johnson resumed working for the STG → calculations for the *Apollo 11* mission to the Moon and Space Shuttle programme

3 Characters

Main characters

Katherine Goble (*later:* Johnson)

- Katherine is a **maths prodigy**, whose extraordinary talent has been promoted from childhood.
- Katherine is **quiet** and **reserved**, but also **tough** and **hardworking**.
- **Widowed with three children**, she tries very hard to combine her demanding job with her family responsibilities.
- At NASA, she performs calculations for John Glenn's *Friendship 7* mission and, by that, contributes significantly to its success.
- She endures the discriminatory behaviour and envy of the STG's white staff (taken for a cleaner, separate coffee pot, disapproving looks, blacked-out figures, etc.).
- Although she **bears much unfair treatment**, she eventually explodes and **makes her point** when she cannot take any more.
- Similarly, she is **self-confident** and makes a stand against patronising Colonel Johnson when they first meet.

Dorothy Vaughan

- Dorothy is **practical** (can repair the car), **self-confident** and firm in her decisions (assigning jobs to her staff).
- She is the **competent leader** of the female computers at Langley.
- Although she **feels underestimated** in her job, she does not rebel, but speaks her mind.
- She is **tough** and puts up with Mrs Mitchell's haughty behaviour.
- Dorothy is **determined** and **knows what she wants** (IBM job).
- To achieve her aim, she **shows initiative** (takes book from public library) and teaches herself the new programming language.
- She encourages Mary to follow her example and act (petition the court) instead of complaining.

Mary Jackson

- Mary has a bachelor's degree in mathematics and physical science.
- She works in Dorothy's "colored" group and is assigned to the engineering department of Mr Zielinski.
- She is **smart**, **quick-witted** and always has an answer (to the white policeman, to Mr Zielinski).
- She is **aware of her potential** and **eager to advance** but hesitates to make the decisive move because of her skin colour.
- Due to Dorothy's and Mr Zielinski's encouragement, however, Mary takes up the fight (motto: further education to overcome racial inequality).
- She is **clever and shrewd** when reasoning with the judge that he should allow her to enrol at a segregated high school ("the first").
- As the only black and female student she is **undeterred** and bravely confronts the suspicious looks of an all-white male class.

Al Harrison

- Harrison is the **leader** of NASA's **Space Task Group**.
- He is **very patriotic**, **highly motivated** and dedicated to his mission of putting an American into space to win the race against the Russians.
- To accomplish the task, he works very hard, and as unrelenting and demanding leader of the STG, he pushes his team to its limits.
- He is **honest** (no extra pay for more work), **open**, **fair and unprejudiced** (abolishes segregated restrooms and coffee pot).
- Harrison feels sorry when he has to dismiss Katherine, as he recognises and appreciates her outstanding contributions.

Minor characters

Paul Stafford
- lead engineer in Al Harrison's Space Task Group
- prejudiced, condescending and envious of Katherine

Vivian Mitchell
- supervisor of Dorothy's "colored computers" group
- prejudiced against African Americans, rather cold and brusque
- Dorothy's achievements and behaviour make her change her ways

Karl Zielinski
- engineer, Polish Jew
- at NASA, responsible for the development of the Mercury capsule
- recognises Mary's talent, becomes her mentor

John Glenn
- first American to orbit the Earth
- national hero
- trusts Katherine's calculations more than those of the IBM machine

Colonel Jim Johnson
- member of the National Guard
- puts his foot in it with Katherine when he first meets her (voices scepticism about women's mathematical abilities)
- persistent → can win Katherine over, marries her

Levi Jackson
- Mary's husband
- supporter of the Civil Rights Movement
- disagrees with Mary on how to deal with racial inequality
- warns his wife not to let NASA use her, but later supports her efforts for further education

4 Themes and interpretation

The themes dealt with in *Hidden Figures* relate to the major topics "discrimination and equality in the world of work" and "The American Dream".

Gender disparities in the world of work

The American Dream promotes the **ideal of economic success and equal opportunities for everyone**. According to the concept, you can become whatever you want if only you work hard enough. In reality, however, this does not seem to apply to all members of society. In the 1960s, the time when the film takes place, more women than ever were entering the paid workforce. Yet, many **working women** had to deal with problems, such as:

- **difficulties in combining work and family** (double burden of household and profession, both of which are time-consuming and stressful),
- **gender stereotyping, prejudices and discrimination** (stereotype of man as breadwinner and woman as homemaker still prevalent, women believed not to be qualified enough for many jobs),
- **the lack of promotion opportunities** (official reason: being unqualified; actual reasons: part-time work, women believed to be too soft for harsh business world, men believed to be superior, etc.).

Being an African American woman made the situation even worse. Even though the percentage of women in the world of work is higher today than it was in the 1960s, working women are generally still facing more difficulties than men.

depiction in the film

difficulties in combining work and family

- Katherine works long hours in her demanding position, lucky to have her mother help with her three daughters; children miss their mum and complain about her being away so long
- Levi subtly reproaches Mary for neglecting her role as housewife and mother ("Kids need to eat their vegetables. You'd know that if you was ever home." Setting 8)

gender stereotyping, prejudices and discrimination

- police officer is surprised that NASA hires women
- Katherine is taken for a cleaning woman when she enters STG office for the first time, puzzled looks by all-white male staff
- initially, Levi does not believe that Mary can overcome obstacles set up by the system ("A female engineer? We're Negro, baby. Ain't no such thing. [...] NASA's never ever given you gals your due. Having a couple of extra degrees ain't gonna change that." Setting 8)
- Colonel Jim Johnson suspects that the NASA job might be too demanding for a woman ("That's pretty heady stuff. They let women handle that sort of ...", setting 8)
- Stafford blacks out information before giving calculations to Katherine ("The rest is classified. You don't have clearance." Setting 6), disparaging remark when Katherine complains ("Those numbers have already been confirmed by two engineers in this department and myself. This is more or less a dummy check." Setting 10)
- Stafford does not accept Katherine's name on reports ("Computers don't author reports." Setting 23)
- Katherine cannot do her work effectively without having data and information as soon as it is available; Stafford is still against her getting access to Pentagon briefings ("Pentagon briefings are not for civilians. It requires the highest clearance. [...] And she is a woman. There is no protocol for a woman attending these meetings." Setting 26)

lack of promotion opportunities

- Dorothy's application for the position as supervisor is rejected without actual explanation (MRS MITCHELL: "Well, that's NASA, for ya. Fast with rocket ships, slow with advancement." Setting 4); Dorothy has been doing the work of a supervisor for almost a year, she thinks she deserves promotion ("I haven't been late one day in ten years. Haven't been out sick. Haven't complained. My work's on time. It's done right. It's done well. [...] What's not fair is having the responsibility of a supervisor but not the title or the pay." Setting 7)
- Mary is refused admission into engineer training programme (MRS MITCHELL: "NASA doesn't commission females for the engineer training programme." Setting 13); new requirements → Mary suspects it is company policy to prevent promotion for women ("Every time we have a chance to get ahead, they move the finish line." Setting 13); Mrs Mitchell warns the women not to question or protest against company policy ("There are no special circumstances for anyone. Y'all should be thankful you have jobs at all." Setting 13)

Racial segregation

The American Dream also promised personal self-realisation in an open society where **equality and liberty** are **guaranteed for all**. For African Americans, however, things were different. Discriminatory laws, also known as "**Jim Crow laws**", resulted in **racial segregation** that was practised in all walks of life. In 1896, the US Supreme Court upheld these discriminatory practices when officially allowing "**separate but equal**" **facilities** to keep the races apart. The repeal of "separate but equal" laws was a major focus of the **Civil Rights Movement**. In 1954, the Supreme Court ruled that segregated schools were unconstitutional (Brown v. Board of Education), but reality still looked different. Racial segregation was not officially prohibited until the passing of the **Civil Rights Act** in 1964.

depiction in the film

segregated seating on buses

- Katherine warns the impatient Mary (who worries about being late for work) that she can walk “or sit in the back of the bus” (setting 2)
- Dorothy and her boys sit in the back of a bus after leaving the library (sign: “For colored patrons only”, setting 15)

segregated schools

- 1926: Katherine’s parents move the family so that their daughter can attend “the best school for Negroes in the state” (setting 1)
- 1961: Hampton High School is still a segregated school (MARY: “Virginia acts like Brown v. Board of Education never happened.” Setting 14), Mary cannot just take classes there but has to fight for admission in court and convince the judge (JUDGE: “Virginia, still a segregated state. Regardless of what the federal government says, regardless of what the Supreme Court says, our law is the law.” Setting 22); she is finally allowed to attend an all-white school, but only the night classes

further segregated facilities and services

- libraries: Dorothy illegally goes to white section of the public library (WOMAN: “You have books in the colored section.” DOROTHY: “It doesn’t have what I’m looking for.” WOMAN: “Well, that’s just the way it is.” Setting 15); thrown out by security, Dorothy tells her sons that “separate and equal are two different things” (setting 15)
- court: separate entrance (sign: “Colored entrance”), segregated seating in courtroom (COURT RECEPTIONIST: “Colored seats are at the back of the courtroom.” Setting 17)
- bathrooms: “colored ladies room” in a separate building (KATHERINE: “There are no colored bathrooms in this building or any building outside the West Campus, which is half a mile away.” Setting 18), Harrison ends segregation by taking down sign (“Here at NASA, we all pee the same color.” Setting 18)
- two separate recreation rooms at Langley Research Center
- separate coffee pot labelled “Colored” for Katherine
- two separate water dispensers in front of ice cream shop

Plot Development in ***Hidden Figures***

	gender and racial discrimination, automation (IBM) ↓	personal initiative and stamina (+ supportive others) ↓	
	main obstacles	**steps taken**	**mission completed**
Katherine	• denied access to relevant information (blacked-out figures, not allowed to take part in briefings) • envied/discriminated against by co-workers (e.g. “colored” coffee pot, not allowed to put her name on report) • loses time (because “colored ladies room” is in another building)	• works long and very hard • vents her anger about unfair treatment • looks for ways to gain necessary information • impresses superiors with outstanding mathematical abilities	plays an essential part in the success of John Glenn's *Friendship 7* mission
Dorothy	• denied official promotion/better pay • fears being replaced by IBM	• learns new programming language • secretly trains herself to use IBM	becomes supervisor of IBM Computing Lab
Mary	• not admitted to engineer training programme • high school still segregated	• goes to court and convinces judge to let her attend classes at high school • gains the necessary qualifications	becomes an engineer

Richard III

1 Key facts about the play

- **author:** William Shakespeare (1564–1616)
- **year of writing:** around 1593
- **year of publication:** 1597 (First Quarto), 1623 (First Folio)
- **genre:** history play
- **structure:** five acts
- **language:** blank verse (traditional in Elizabethan dramas), i. e. lines do not rhyme, metre: iambic pentameter (five feet to each line, each foot contains two beats, with the stress on the second beat)
- **setting:** England between 1471 and 1485
- **content:** Richard of Gloucester, later King Richard III, sets out on a bloody crusade to usurp the English crown. He eliminates any opposition until he is eventually killed by the Earl of Richmond.
- **historical background:** Wars of the Roses (1455–1485): series of civil wars for the throne of England between two competing royal families (the House of York and the House of Lancaster); end: Henry Tudor, Earl of Richmond, defeated Richard III and became King Henry VII; his marriage to Elizabeth of York united the two sides and ended the fighting

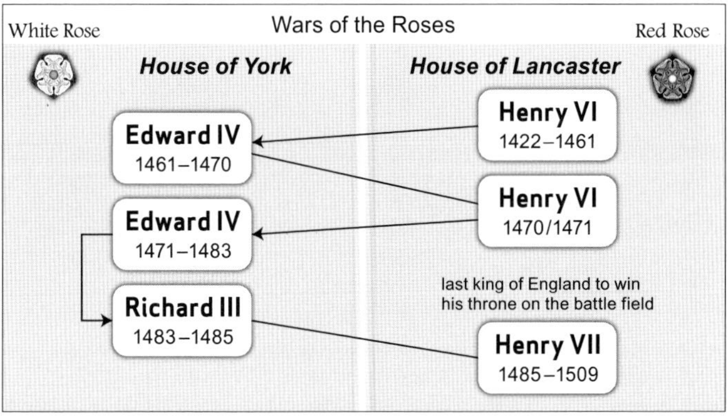

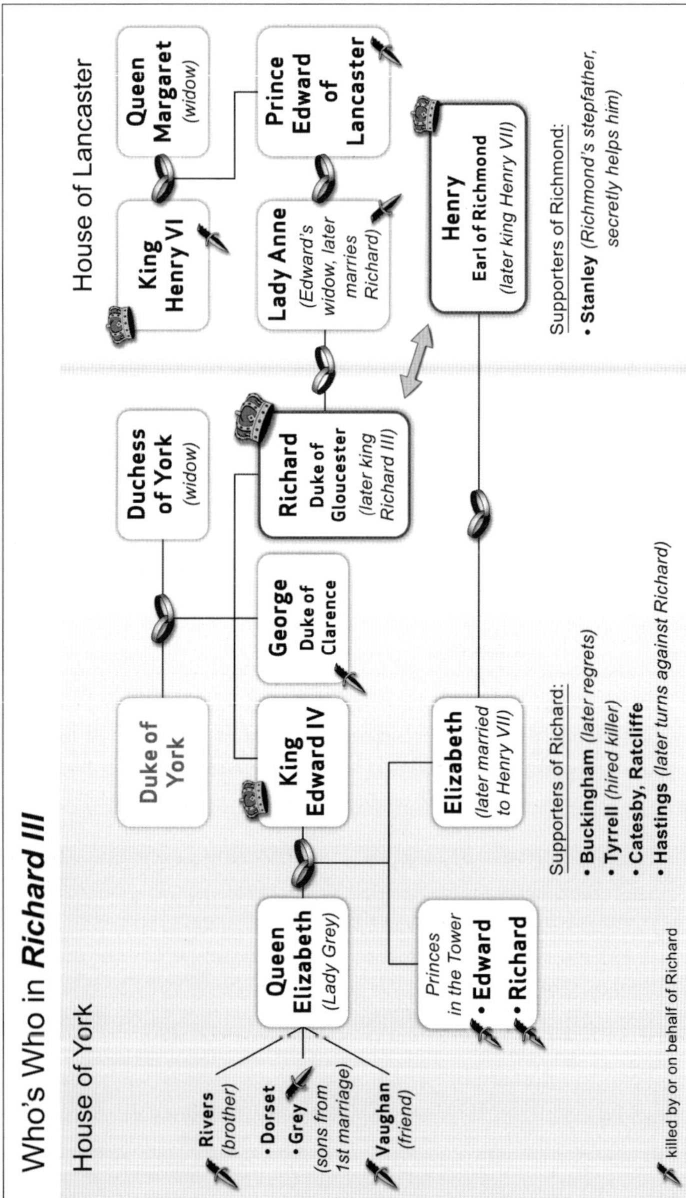

Who's Who in Richard III
House of York
House of Lancaster
Rivers (brother)
• Dorset
• Grey
(sons from 1st marriage)
Vaughan (friend)
Queen Elizabeth (Lady Grey)
Princes in the Tower
• Edward
• Richard
Duke of York
King Edward IV
Elizabeth (later married to Henry VII)
George Duke of Clarence
Duchess of York (widow)
Richard Duke of Gloucester (later king Richard III)
King Henry VI
Queen Margaret (widow)
Lady Anne (Edward's widow, later marries Richard)
Prince Edward of Lancaster
Henry Earl of Richmond (later king Henry VII)
Supporters of Richard:
• Buckingham (later regrets)
• Tyrrell (hired killer)
• Catesby, Ratcliffe
• Hastings (later turns against Richard)
Supporters of Richmond:
• Stanley (Richmond's stepfather, secretly helps him)
killed by or on behalf of Richard

2 Key facts about the film

- **screenplay:** Ian McKellen (*1939 in Burnley, England) and Richard Loncraine (*1946 in Cheltenham, England), based on Shakespeare's play
- **director:** Richard Loncraine
- **release date:** 1995
- **awards:** Silver Bear for Best Director (1996), BAFTA Film Award for Best Production Design and for Best Costume Design (both in 1997)
- **running time:** ca. 104 minutes
- **setting:** 1930s England
- **changes to the play:**
  Richard III is one of Shakespeare's longest plays → had to be shortened for the film version:
  - characters deleted (e. g. Margaret, bishops), important information transferred to other characters
  - dialogues cut (e. g. Richard and Anne; women's rhetorised grief in Act IV)

  further changes, e. g.:
  - film's action begins earlier: with assassination of King Henry VI
  - in the play, Clarence has children (son Edward, Earl of Warwick, and daughter Margaret Plantagenet, Countess of Salisbury) ↔ in the film, he is childless (reason: too many other children would distract from the young princes and their fate in the Tower)
  - Queen Elizabeth and her brother Earl Rivers speak with an American accent to denote that they come from a family which is only mid-ranked in the English aristocracy
  - adaptions to the 1930s: places (ballroom, morgue, urinal, battle field, etc.), clothing (soldiers in SS-like uniforms, gas masks), weaponry (guns, tanks), means of transport (cars, airplanes), devices (telegraph, typewriter, camera)

3 Plot

Act I[2]

Act I, Scene 1 **a street in London**

- recent victory of the Yorkists in civil war between the royal families → King Edward IV takes the throne again
- the king's younger brother Richard, Duke of Gloucester, is convinced that he is not made for peaceful times (due to his physical deformity, he cannot be a good lover) → determined to be a villain instead
- Richard reveals: he has already hatched a plot to drive a wedge between his two brothers and get rid of them
- Richard's brother George, Duke of Clarence, is escorted to prison (reason: king believes a prophecy – spread by Richard – that someone whose name starts with "G" will usurp the throne) → Richard plays the innocent, promises Clarence to help him
- Richard hears that the king is sick → hopes that Clarence will be executed before the king dies
- Richard reveals his plan to marry Lady Anne, whose father-in-law (King Henry VI) and husband (Prince Edward) he had killed

Act I, Scene 2 **another street in London**

- funeral procession for dead King Henry VI: Lady Anne mourns the deaths of her father-in-law and her husband, curses their murderer
- Richard first denies having killed her husband, then claims that the reason for his deed was her beauty
- Richard courts Lady Anne → she feels flattered, accepts Richard's ring and allows him to see her again
- when alone, Richard boasts about having manipulated Anne

Act I, Scene 3 **London, a room in the palace**

- Queen Elizabeth worries about her husband's health
- her fear: their two sons are too young to rule → if king dies, Richard will control throne until her and Edward's oldest son comes of age

2 Depicted is the plot and structure of the play, not the film version, based on the bilingual Reclam edition (2014, edited by Herbert Geisen).

- news: the king is doing better, wishes to reconcile Richard with Elizabeth's relatives → sends for them
- Richard insists that he is an honest and virtuous man → insinuation: people at court slander him
- Richard accuses Elizabeth of being responsible for Clarence's imprisonment, argument between them escalates
- Queen Margaret (Henry VI's widow) returns from exile and curses everyone in the room: Richard will bring the House of York bad luck, he and all who make a pact with him will pay for it
- Richard hires two murderers to kill his brother Clarence

Act I, Scene 4 | **Tower of London**

- the Duke of Clarence, imprisoned in the Tower of London, foresaw his death in a bad dream the night before
- Richard's hired murderers arrive, hand Brackenbury (lieutenant of Tower) a warrant issued in the name of the king → Brackenbury leaves
- murderers discuss how best to kill Clarence
- Clarence suddenly wakes up and pleads with murderers
- one murderer hesitates (due to moral scruples), but the other stabs Clarence and drowns him in a keg of wine

Act II

Act II, Scene 1 | **London, a room in the palace**

- news of Clarence's death comes as a great shock because King Edward had actually issued a pardon
- Richard claims: cancellation of sentence was delivered too slowly
- King Edward blames himself for his brother's death
- suffering from grief and guilt, he grows sicker again

Act II, Scene 2 | **London, a room in the palace**

- Duchess of York knows how evil her son Richard really is and that he killed his brother → she grieves that she ever gave birth to him
- Queen Elizabeth announces King Edward's death
- Dorset and Rivers advise Queen Elizabeth to have her son, Prince Edward (12 years old), crowned as soon as possible

Act II, Scene 3 | **a street in London**

- three ordinary citizens meet in the street and worry about the turmoil which might occur after King Edward's death

Act II, Scene 4 | **London, a room in the palace**

- the Duchess of York, her daughter-in-law (Queen Elizabeth) and her grandson (the young Duke of York) await Prince Edward's return
- news: Rivers, Grey (Elizabeth's relatives) and Vaughan (an ally of theirs) are imprisoned on the orders of Richard and Buckingham
- Queen Elizabeth foresees the "ruin of [her] house"
- knowing that Richard means her ill, she decides to flee with her youngest son and hide in a secret place

Act III

Act III, Scene 1 | **a street in London**

- young Prince Edward arrives in London and learns that his mother and his brother have taken sanctuary
- Buckingham orders Cardinal Bourchier and Hastings to retrieve young York from Elizabeth, if necessary by force
- Richard advises Prince Edward and his brother to hide until Edward's coronation → although both princes do not like the idea, Richard sends them off to the Tower of London
- Richard's promise: after he becomes king, he will give Buckingham the title of Earl of Hereford

Act III, Scene 2 | **London, in front of Lord Hastings' house**

- after a nightmare, Stanley fears for his and Hastings' safety → suggests fleeing to the north, but Hastings ignores the warning
- Catesby arrives to find out Hastings' feelings about Richard's scheme → brings up the idea that Richard should take the crown instead of Prince Edward → Hastings reacts shocked

Act III, Scene 3 | **Pomfret, in front of the castle**

- Rivers, Grey and Vaughan expect their execution
- they realise that Queen Margaret's curse against them has come true

Act III, Scene 4	Tower of London

- fake council session: Hastings, Stanley and others gather to discuss the date of Edward's coronation (that's what they think)
- Richard blames Queen Elizabeth and Hastings' mistress Shore for his deformation (he claims that they must have cast a spell on him)
- Richard accuses Hastings of treachery → orders his execution
- Hastings laments having disregarded Stanley's warning

Act III, Scene 5	London, the Tower walls

- Richard and Buckingham make the mayor of London believe that Hastings was a traitor and that Richard was right to have him executed
- Richard sends Buckingham to make speeches to the people of London: supposed to make them turn against the princes (implying that they aren't even Edward's legitimate heirs)
- Richard plans to have Clarence's children removed
- he forbids access to the princes in the Tower

Act III, Scene 6	a street in London

- a scrivener who has a copied indictment of Hastings knows that the claim on paper is a lie invented by Richard
- he is willing to keep quiet about his discovery

Act III, Scene 7	London, the court of Baynard's castle

- Buckingham reports: speech to the Londoners was received badly
- strategy: urge the mayor to beg Richard to be king, pretending that this request would represent the will of the people
- at first, Richard pretends not to be interested but eventually gives in, seemingly unwillingly, to comply with the people's wishes
- the coronation is to take place the following day

Act IV

Act IV, Scene 1	in front of the Tower of London

- Queen Elizabeth, the Duchess of York and Lady Anne (now Richard's wife) are not allowed to visit the princes in the Tower

- Anne fears that Richard's coronation will mean ruin for England and regrets not having resisted marrying him
- she remembers that she herself has cursed Richard and his future wife earlier (cf. I, 2)
- Dorset heads off to Earl of Richmond, Elizabeth returns to sanctuary

Act IV, Scene 2 | **London, a room of state in the palace**

- King Richard does not yet feel safe in his position → tells Buckingham that he wishes the two princes to be murdered in the Tower
- Buckingham hesitates → Richard hires James Tyrrell
- Richard tells Catesby to spread the rumour that Anne is fatally ill
- he announces his intention to marry his niece, the young Elizabeth of York
- Richard ignores Buckingham's request for the earldom of Hereford which Richard had promised him earlier (cf. III, 1)
- Buckingham remembers the fate of Richard's other enemies → flees

Act IV, Scene 3 | **London, a room of state in the palace**

- Tyrrell reports: the two young princes are dead
- Richard announces (to the audience): he has locked up Clarence's son, he has married off Clarence's daughter to an unimportant man, his wife Anne has died
- Richard must make progress with his plan to marry Elizabeth before the Earl of Richmond (who wants to marry her too) gets there first

Act IV, Scene 4 | **London, in front of the palace**

- Elizabeth and the Duchess of York lament the deaths of the young princes and all the others murdered at the behest of Richard
- the Duchess of York curses her son Richard to die bloodily
- Richard reveals to the former queen Elizabeth that he wants to marry her daughter → Elizabeth is horrified
- Richard tries to sweet-talk Elizabeth and argues that the marriage is the only way the kingdom can avoid a civil war → she seems to be persuaded
- news: Richmond has landed in England with a powerful army, more and more noblemen join the rebel forces, Buckingham has been captured; Richard and his men prepare for battle

Act IV, Scene 5 | **London, a room in Lord Stanley's house**

- Stanley would like to change sides and support the rebel leader Richmond, but he cannot because Richard is holding his son hostage
- Elizabeth has agreed that her daughter should marry Richmond, not Richard

Act V

Act V, Scene 1 | **Salisbury, an open place**

- on the way to his execution, Buckingham remembers Margaret's prophecy → realises that he deserves punishment for his crimes (being accomplice to murder) and for his foolishness in trusting Richard

Act V, Scene 2 | **a plain near Tamworth**

- Richmond encourages his troops to fight against the tyrant Richard

Act V, Scene 3 | **Bosworth Field**

- both sides prepare for battle the next day
- Richard is confident because his army is larger than Richmond's
- Richard and Richmond are asleep; the ghosts of everyone whom Richard has murdered appear: Prince Edward (Henry VI's son), Henry VI, Richard's brother Clarence, Rivers, Grey and Vaughan, Hastings, the two young princes, Lady Anne, Buckingham → first, each ghost condemns Richard, then praises and blesses Richmond
- Richard awakes from the bad dream, truly terrified → tries to suppress his fear and calm his conscience
- Richmond feels great, as for him the dream was full of good omens

Act V, Scene 4 | **another part of the field**

- Richard fights courageously, although his horse has been killed
- Richmond kills Richard with his sword and is crowned king
- Richmond, now King Henry VII, announces that Richard's soldiers who have fled will be pardoned if they submit, and that he will marry Elizabeth of York → the two rival royal families will finally be united

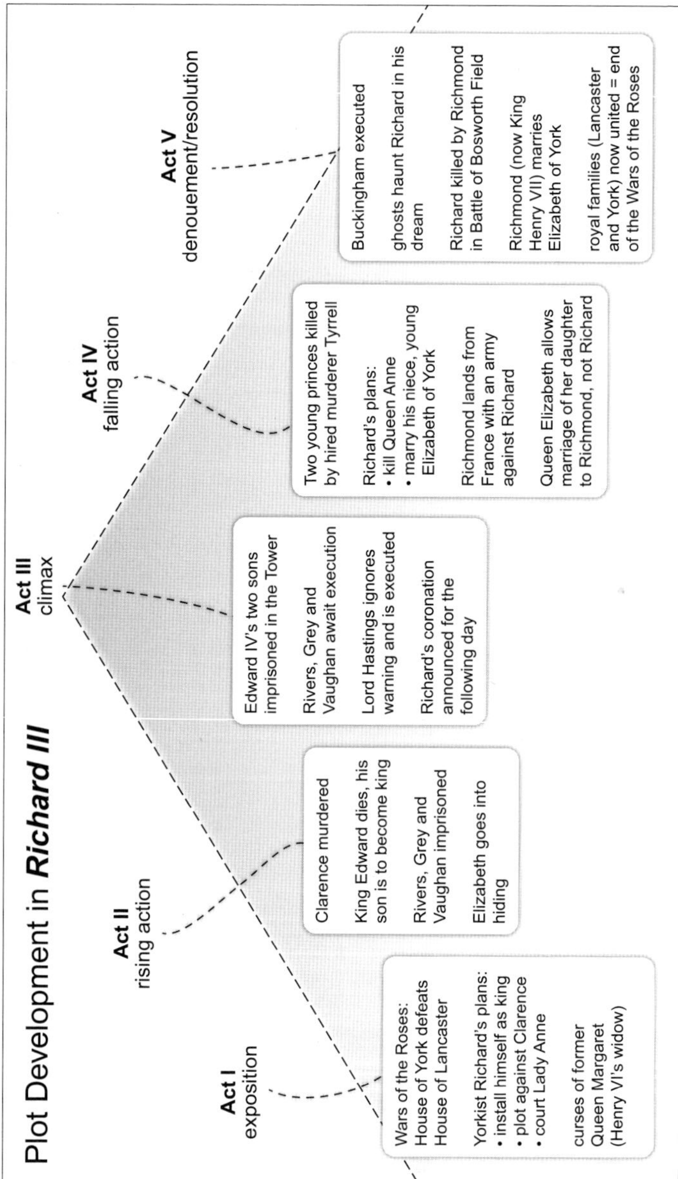
Plot Development in *Richard III*
Act I exposition
Wars of the Roses: House of York defeats House of Lancaster
Yorkist Richard's plans: • install himself as king • plot against Clarence • court Lady Anne
curses of former Queen Margaret (Henry VI's widow)
Act II rising action
Clarence murdered
King Edward dies, his son is to become king
Rivers, Grey and Vaughan imprisoned
Elizabeth goes into hiding
Act III climax
Edward IV's two sons imprisoned in the Tower
Rivers, Grey and Vaughan await execution
Lord Hastings ignores warning and is executed
Richard's coronation announced for the following day
Act IV falling action
Two young princes killed by hired murderer Tyrrell
Richard's plans: • kill Queen Anne • marry his niece, young Elizabeth of York
Richmond lands from France with an army against Richard
Queen Elizabeth allows marriage of her daughter to Richmond, not Richard
Act V denouement/resolution
Buckingham executed
ghosts haunt Richard in his dream
Richard killed by Richmond in Battle of Bosworth Field
Richmond (now King Henry VII) marries Elizabeth of York
royal families (Lancaster and York) now united = end of the Wars of the Roses

4 Characters

Main characters

Richard

- Richard, initially Duke of Gloucester and later King Richard III, is a member of the **House of York**.
- He is **physically deformed** (he has a hunchback and a withered arm) and very **ugly**.
- Richard is **bitter** about his physical deformity and uses it as his justification for playing "the villain".
- Richard is **over-ambitious** and **power-hungry:** to achieve his aim of seizing the English crown, he uses a cunning scheme and renounces any normal ethics and morality.
- He is a **deceitful**, **cruel** and **malicious** person, a **hideous** monster without any scruples.
- He is **cold** and **calculating:** he uses people and gets rid of them once they have fulfilled their function in his plot (e. g. Buckingham and Lady Anne).
- Richard is an **excellent speaker**, **charming in words**, and a **manipulative liar**, who manages to sweet-talk and persuade other people, even those who actually hate him.

Duke of Buckingham

- Buckingham is **Richard's loyal ally** and right-hand man.
- He is almost as **amoral** as Richard himself.
- Being **ambitious** and **greedy** for power and wealth, he ignores Queen Margaret's warning ("O Buckingham! take heed of yonder dog", I, 3[3]) and supports Richard's evil plans blindly, because he is promised the earldom of Hereford for his service.
- When Buckingham **realises his error** and flees, it is **too late:** he is captured and beheaded.
- Before he dies, he confesses and repents.

3 The numbers given at the end of a quotation refer to the act and the scene in the bilingual Reclam edition.

Henry Tudor, Earl of Richmond

- Richmond, nephew to King Henry VI and later King Henry VII, is a member of the **House of Lancaster**.
- He is **Richard's opponent**.
- In contrast to Richard, he is an **upright** character.
- He is a **bold**, **powerful** and **fair** leader with a **legitimate claim to the throne**.
- After defeating the tyrant Richard, he marries Elizabeth of York, daughter of King Edward, thus causing the Wars of the Roses to end.

Queen Margaret

- Queen Margaret is the widow of King Henry VI.
- She grieves the deaths of her husband Henry and her son Edward and is determined to make the living pay for her losses.
- She is **bitter**, **sharp-tongued** and **revengeful**.
- She prophesises doom and misery for Richard and his supporters (I, 3) and eventually **sees her curses and prophecies fulfilled**.
- Although she appears in just two scenes (I, 3 and IV, 4), she is an important **antagonist to Richard**.

Queen Elizabeth

- Queen Elizabeth is the wife of King Edward IV.
- Richard falsely blames her for being responsible for Clarence's imprisonment.
- She is **deeply shocked** by the cruel murder of her two young sons.
- Although she becomes aware that Richard is behind the misdeeds, she **yields to Richard's flattery** and agrees to his marrying her daughter.
- In Richard's eyes, this makes her a "[r]elenting fool, and shallow changing woman" (IV, 4).
- However, she changes her mind (daughter Elizabeth is to marry Richmond), which makes her appear **wiser and stronger than Richard thought**.

Duchess of York

- The Duchess of York is mother to King Edward IV, George, Duke of Clarence and Richard, Duke of Gloucester.
- She has **endured grief** most of her life and mourns the violent deaths of her husband and her son Clarence.
- She suffers because she knows that she is the **mother of the monstrous Richard** ("He is my son, ay, and therein my shame", II, 2).
- She denies him the blessing he hypocritically asks for.
- Her plea to God that Richard may reform remains unfulfilled.

Lady Anne

- Lady Anne is the widow of Edward, Prince of Wales (son to King Henry VI) and later becomes Richard's wife.
- She **mourns** the death of Edward and indulges in self-pity.
- She appears **confused**, **emotionally unstable** and **weak**.
- Knowing Richard's past evils, she initially resists his approach, but eventually lets herself be **won over by his flattery**.
- Later, she suspects Richard's plots against her.
- She regrets her marriage and hates Richard until her premature death.

Minor characters

King Edward IV

- older brother of Richard and Clarence, king of England at the beginning of the play
- tries to reconcile his and his wife's families
- unaware that Richard is attempting to usurp his place

George, Duke of Clarence

- Richard's older brother and first victim (because he stands ahead in the line of succession to the throne)
- too gentle, trusting and unsuspecting
- refuses to believe that his own brother has plotted against him

Lord Hastings

- loyal supporter of King Edward IV
- naive and trusting: recently released from prison, he believes Richard's protestations that Queen Elizabeth (widow of Edward IV) was responsible for his imprisonment
- thinks that he and his friend Stanley are safe in the favour of Richard and Buckingham and thus ignores Stanley's warning
- realises too late that Richard has ambitions to be king
- when he gives Richard's ally Catesby to understand that he would never support Richard as king, Richard has him assassinated

Lord Stanley

- foresees the danger that Richard will bring in a dream (III, 2); warns his friend Hastings
- tries not to offend Richard, but secretly helps his stepson Richmond

The two young princes

- Prince Edward and Richard, Duke of York (sons of King Edward IV and his wife, Elizabeth)
- after Edward's death, the young Prince Edward is the rightful heir to the throne
- their uncle Richard has them locked up and murdered in the tower

Rivers, Dorset and Grey

- relatives and allies of King Edward's wife, Queen Elizabeth
- Earl Rivers is Elizabeth's brother; the Marquess of Dorset and Lord Grey are her sons from her first marriage
- Richard has Rivers and Grey executed, Dorset can flee

Sir James Tyrrell

- a murderer hired by Richard to kill the two young princes
- willing to do anything for money

5 Themes and interpretation

The themes dealt with in *Richard III* relate to the major topics "the pursuit of power", "the role(s) of women" and "fate vs. free will".

The pursuit of power

Shakespeare's representation of Richard's rise to power is strongly influenced by literary, political and historical contexts.

Background information

vice figure	The character of Richard can be seen in the tradition of the medieval **morality plays** in which the protagonists were personifications of moral aberrations. The so-called **vice figure** was a personification of senseless evil and a master of deception who often let the audience in on his/her plans.
Machiavellian politics	In his handbook *The Prince* (1513), Niccolò Machiavelli promoted a political philosophy that was also known to Elizabethan playwrights. "Machiavellian" politics was often associated with cunning, **manipulative behaviour** and **brilliant rhetoric**; "Machiavellian" characters are usually presented as **power-hungry individuals without any moral scruples**.
ambition as a character flaw	The representation of an **extreme will to power** as the protagonist's **fatal flaw** also appears in other Shakespeare plays, such as *Macbeth*. However, whereas Macbeth is vexed by scruples and doubts, Richard reveals a troubled conscience rather late in his final, alarming soliloquy.
Tudor myth	The "Tudor myth" is the idea that the rise of the Tudor dynasty led to a period of peace, unity and prosperity for England, ending the chaos and bloodshed of the Wars of the Roses. It can thus be seen as **political propaganda** that served to glorify Tudor rule. In line with this notion, Shakespeare presents the Yorkist Richard III as a hideous monster and incarnation of evil, who was luckily defeated by the Tudor Henry VII (grandfather of Elizabeth I, who ruled during Shakespeare's time).

depiction in the play

Richard's motives

- in his opening soliloquy (I, 1), Richard confides to the audience that he is dissatisfied with a life "in this weak piping time of peace" and with his physical deformity which does not qualify him as a lover

- thus, he has decided "to prove a villain", as some kind of compensation or revenge for the misfortunes of nature

Richard's evil plans

- similar to the medieval vice figure, Richard discloses the evil methods he is going to use to the audience
- after King Henry VI's death, he puts his plan to seize the throne into action, using his rhetorical power and skills in dissimulation
- his greed for personal power makes him disregard any moral considerations and limitations, making him a Machiavellian villain
  - he has no scruples to first eliminate those who stand before him in the line of the crown (his older brother Clarence and his two child nephews); he deceives the mourning widow Anne, whose husband and father-in-law he had killed
  - his pursuit for power and insatiable ambition makes him unfeeling and cruel (he ignores the desperate appeals of his own mother, the Duchess of York, and snubs the suffering of his sister-in-law, Queen Elizabeth, whose sons he has killed)
  - when he becomes king, Richard takes measures to secure his position by removing those who do not support him and whose "services" are no longer needed
  - the killing of Buckingham, who had served him for a long time, further enhances the image of Richard as the despicable personification of immorality and evil

depiction in the film

Richard's motives

- in his introduction to the screenplay[4], actor and screenwriter Ian McKellen argues that he does not see Richard as inherently evil; rather, Richard's wickedness is "an outcome of other people's disaffection with his physique" → from infancy Richard was exposed to verbal and emotional abuse and this has formed his character and behaviour

4 All quotes on this and the next page are taken from the following website: http://www.mckellen.com/cinema/richard/screenplay/index.htm

- consequently, the film presents Richard as a person on a crusade who takes vengeance on a society that has always treated him as an outsider; however, he still remains a vicious, hideous criminal
- in numerous scenes Richard talks to the camera, letting the viewers in on his secret plans (e.g. in the urinal; by the Thames when he sees his brother George off to the tower; at the breakfast table when he regrets that Clarence is still alive)

Richard as a fascist leader

- the film version transfers the action to the 1930s and associates Richard with the rise of fascism (SS-like uniforms; flags in colours similar to those of the Nazis; cheering masses, etc.)
- McKellen explains this decision as follows: "The historical events of the play had occurred just a couple of generations before the first audience saw them dramatised. The comparable period for us would be the 1930s […]. Also, the '30s were appropriately a decade of tyranny throughout Europe, the most recent time when a dictatorship like Richard III's might have overtaken the United Kingdom"
- this setting has the advantage of allowing for multiple interpretations with diverse audiences: "In Hamburg, Richard's blackshirt troops seemed like a commentary on the Third Reich. In Bucharest, when Richard was slain, the Romanians stopped the show with heartfelt cheers, in memory of their recent freedom from Ceaucescu's regime. In Cairo, as the Gulf War was hotting up, it all seemed like a new play about Saddam Hussein."

The role(s) of women

During Shakespeare's time, women were **socially and financially dependent** on men and expected to obey their husbands (one of the most prominent exceptions being the "Virgin Queen" Elizabeth I, who was unmarried and ruled the country for over 40 years). In the Elizabethan theatre, women were not allowed on stage, so the female characters had to be played by boy actors.

The *dramatis personae* of *Richard III* lists five female characters (Queen Elizabeth, Queen Margaret, the Duchess of York, Lady Anne and Lady Margaret Plantagenet), who play an ambivalent role.

depiction in the play

- generally speaking, the women in *Richard III* are **bystanders** who comment on evil occurrences and forecast disasters but are unable to influence the course of events; in this sense they can be compared to the choir in classic Greek tragedies – they warn, but their warnings go unheard
- they are the innocent **sufferers of losses**, the victims of Richard's vivacious plots and manoeuvres
- Margaret, Anne, and Elizabeth grieve, complain or bury the dead, **reminding** the audience of Richard's **bloody deeds**
- at the same time, the women seem **eerily powerful** in their capacity to **curse** and to **prophesy** events → by the end of the play, most of their curses have come true (see table below)

person(s) cursed	women's curses	curse fulfilled
Edward IV	**Margaret:** Though not by war, by surfeit die your king, / As ours by murder, to make him a king! (I, 3)	Edward IV dies after hearing that the death warrant for his brother George was carried out
young Edward (son of Queen Elizabeth)	**Margaret:** Edward, thy son, that now is Prince of Wales, / For Edward, my son, which was Prince of Wales, / Die in his youth by like untimely violence! (I, 3)	young Edward is killed in the Tower together with his brother Richard
Queen Elizabeth	**Margaret:** Thyself a queen, for me that was a queen, / Outlive thy glory, like my wretched self! / Long mayst thou live to wail thy children's loss (I, 3)	Elizabeth is deeply distressed when her sons, the young prin-ces, are murdered
Rivers, Dorset, Hastings	**Margaret:** Rivers and Dorset, you were standers by, – / And so wast thou, Lord Hastings, – when my son / Was stabb'd with bloody daggers: God, I pray him, / That none of you may live your natural age, / But by some unlook'd accident cut off. (I, 3)	Rivers is executed; Hastings is assas-sinated; only Dorset can flee
Richard Gloucester	**Margaret:** No sleep close up that deadly eye of thine, / Unless it be while some tormenting dream / Affrights thee with a hell of ugly devils! (I, 3)	the night before the battle, ghosts haunt Richard; he is killed in battle the next day

Buckingham	**Margaret:** O Buckingham! take heed of yonder dog: [...] remember this another day, / When he shall split thy very heart with sorrow, / And say poor Margaret was a prophetess. (I, 3)	Buckingham is executed, remembers Margaret's words before his death
Richard Gloucester	**Lady Anne:** O! cursed be the hand that made these holes; / Cursed the heart that had the heart to do it! / Cursed the blood that let this blood from hence! (I, 2)	Richard is killed in battle
Richard's future wife	**Lady Anne:** If ever he have wife, let her be made / More miserable by the death of him / Than I am made by my young lord and thee! (I, 2)	without realising it, Anne curses herself
Richard Gloucester	**Duchess of York:** Bloody thou art, bloody will be thy end; / Shame serves thy life and doth thy death attend. (IV, 4)	Richard is killed in battle

differences in the film

- the film leaves out the role of Queen Margaret (Mc Kellen believed that there would not be enough time in the film to explain clearly who she is and that the viewers would be confused by her jumping back and forth between recent and past events) → the Duchess of York takes over some of Margaret's lines
- Princess Elizabeth, daughter of King Edward and Queen Elizabeth, plays a greater role in the film (in the play she is an offstage character, even though she ends up as Queen of England through her marriage to Henry, Earl of Richmond)

Fate vs. free will

The Renaissance was a time in which different world views coexisted. On the one hand, the view of the individual who can shape his or her destiny was beginning to take hold. At the same time, a lot of people believed that their lives were predetermined by fate or divine Providence. In *Richard III* elements of both concepts can be found.

Background information

free will	– **Machiavellian political philosophy** stressed the notion of free will and an individual who is in full control of his or her life
fatalism	– At the same time, the ancient idea of a "**wheel of fortune**" was still very much alive. It said that Goddess Fortune (Fate) turns her wheel, bringing people from the bottom to the top and letting those at the top fall down again. In other words, those who **rise** to power will inevitably lose their power again and **fall**. – In Christian terms, there was the widespread belief that everything happens according to some greater, **divine plan** and that sinners will ultimately be punished for their deeds (**divine justice**). – On the political plane, the "**Tudor myth**" represented the bloody reign of Richard III as a divine punishment for the overthrow of Richard II and as a necessary phase in history that ultimately led to the glorious rule of the Tudors.

Free will in *Richard III*

- Richard declares that he is "determined to prove a villain" (I, 1); he is confident that he can act of his own free will
- he puts his vicious plans into action to promote his advancement to the throne and secure his position; his Machiavellian schemes work out at the beginning
- when he awakes from the dream in which the ghosts appeared, he berates his conscience for giving him bad dreams ("What! do I fear myself? there's none else by", V, 3)

Fate in *Richard III*

- almost all of the women's curses in the play are eventually fulfilled, suggesting that the events are predetermined by fate (see table on pp. 76/77)
- in IV, 4 Margaret asks God to punish Richard for his perfidiousness and thus execute divine justice: "Cancel his bond of life, dear God! I pray, / That I may live to say, The dog is dead."
- in V, 3, the ghosts representing those whom Richard has killed during his lifetime predict Richard's end ("despair, and die") and Richmond's victory ("live, and flourish") → this likewise seems to hint at a divine plan

- before he is about to die, Buckingham realises his villainy and admits the divine justice in his death ("This, this All-Souls' day to my fearful soul / Is the determin'd respite of my wrongs", V, 1)
- in a dream Clarence foresees his own death, suggesting that it might have been fated: "Lord, Lord! methought what pain it was to drown: / What dreadful noise of water in mine ears!" (I, 4)
- similarly, Stanley foresees the danger posed by Richard in a dream: "this night / He dreamt the boar had razed off his helm" (III, 2)
- Richard wants Queen Elizabeth to believe that the fate of her sons was predetermined: "at their births good stars were opposite! […] All unavoided is the doom of destiny." (IV, 4)

ghosts and their curses in V, 3	reference to passages earlier in the play
Ghost of Prince Edward: Let me sit heavy on thy soul to-morrow! / Think how thou stab'dst me in my prime of youth / At Tewksbury	**Richard:** Edward, her lord, whom I, some three months since, / Stabb'd in my angry mood at Tewksbury (I, 2)
Ghost of King Henry VI: When I was mortal, my anointed body / By thee was punched full of deadly holes	**Richard:** for I did kill King Henry (I, 2)
Ghost of Clarence: Let me sit heavy on thy soul to-morrow! / I, that was wash'd to death with fulsome wine	**Richard:** Clarence hath not another day to live (I, 1)
Ghost of Rivers: Let me sit heavy on thy soul to-morrow! / Rivers, that died at Pomfret! despair, and die! **Ghost of Grey:** Think upon Grey, and let thy soul despair. **Ghost of Vaughan:** Think upon Vaughan, and with guilty fear / Let fall thy pointless lance: despair, and die!	Rivers, Grey and Vaughan are executed in III, 3; **Grey:** Now Margaret's curse is fall'n upon our heads, / When she exclaim'd on Hastings, you, and I, / For standing by when Richard stabb'd her son. (III, 3)
Ghost of Hastings: Bloody and guilty, guiltily awake; / And in a bloody battle end thy days!	**Richard:** Off with his head! (III, 4)
Ghost of the Princes: Dream on thy cousins smother'd in the Tower	**Richard:** I wish the bastards dead (IV, 2)
Ghost of Lady Anne: Richard, thy wife, that wretched Anne thy wife, / That never slept a quiet hour with thee	**Richard:** I'll have her; but I will not keep her long. (I, 2)
Ghost of Buckingham: The first was I that help'd thee to the crown: / The last was I that felt thy tyranny.	**Richard:** Some one take order Buckingham be brought / To Salisbury (IV, 4); execution: V, 1